LIFE IS ALWAYS IN PROGRESS

.... so take the brakes off

LIFE IS ALWAYS IN PROGRESS

.... so take the brakes off

Loretta H. Browning

LIFE IS ALWAYS IN PROGRESS
.... so take the brakes off

All Rights Reserved.
Copyright © 2009 by Loretta H. Browning.
ISBN: 978-0-9762681-6-1

No part of this book may be reproduced or transmitted in any form or by any means, graphic, electronic, or mechanical, including photocopying, recording, taping or by any information storage or retrieval system, without the permission in writing from the publisher.

Unless otherwise indicated, all Scripture quotations are from the KING JAMES VERSION of the Bible.

Published by:
Ronnie J. Wells Publishing
P.O. Box 90151
Atlanta, Georgia 30364
www.ronniejwells.com

Cover Art by: Bella Lane Designs

Printed in the United States of America

Table of Contents

Dedication IV
Preface VI
Introduction VII
Chapter 1 Where Memories Were Made 1
Chapter 2 You've Gotta Show Up 27
Chapter 3 Take Your Mark 47
Chapter 4 Get Set - Go 59
Chapter 5 Pole Position 71
Chapter 6 Marbles 87
Chapter 7 Draft 103
Chapter 8 Bank 123
Chapter 9 Silly Season 139
Chapter 10 Follow the Road Map 151
Epilogue 165
Acknowledgements 178
About the Author 179

Dedication

This book is dedicated to my Heavenly Father for using me as a vessel to encourage those who have chosen to stand on the sidelines and watch life pass them by. It is also dedicated to the memory of my father, John Henry Hunter, and especially my mother, Ruby Lee Hunter, who was my biggest "shero," for without them, there would be no me. They are no longer here, but my love for them remains.

Also, I dedicate this book to my late husband, Cliff Browning, who always encouraged me to do my very best and stay focused. His favorite saying was "People do what they want to do." Those words have given me the determination to strive for the things that God has predestined for my life.

To my two adorable daughters, Terra LaShon Smiley and Thomi LaShea Breedlove, and my sons-in-law, I love you.

Also, to my five grandchildren: Victoria, Tarance, Elizabeth, William and Tyler. I love you so much because you're my five wonders of the world. I hope that as you progress in your life, you will hold God to His promise. It is my prayer that you make a statement that will be recorded in God's Kingdom and change the history of the world. I pray that you will make your mark, take the brakes off and live a glorious life that has been predestined just for you. Know, though, that you cannot do it alone.

"For it is in Christ that we find out who we are and what we are living for. Long before we first heard of Christ, he had his eye on us, had designs on us for glorious living, part of the overall purpose he is working out in everything and everyone."
~~Ephesians 1:11 (Msg)

And finally, this book is dedicated to people like me—those who feel that there is more on the inside of them which will be revealed in due time. God is getting ready to set you before people whom you never thought you would encounter in this lifetime. It is not by accident that you and I have been chosen to connect at this appointed time in our lives. The mere fact that you are holding this book in your hands at this very moment is an indication that you have put yourself in a position to be blessed.

My prayer is that this reading will be a "lamp unto your feet and a light unto your path" (Psalm 119:105). May this book bless your spirit and assist you in paving the way to the simple, stress-free life that is full of purpose with a direct relationship to the Kingdom of God. So take the brakes off, keep moving—and happy reading.

Preface

Do you sometimes feel defeated, frustrated, and disappointed with life? Do you feel that you have all that you could possibly need or even want, but there's still a big void? King Solomon, the richest man that ever lived, spoke of this over 3000 years ago. He had a large home and many wives, but he summarized all his efforts of finding life's meaning as "chasing the wind" because he realized that regardless of what he had, he always wanted more. After searching and searching, he eventually realized that a life without God is not worth living.

Like King Solomon, some people are dissatisfied and tend to be going in circles. They have not found their purpose in life. Have you? Do you feel that even though God has blessed you with material wealth, you really are not happy? I have found that our true purpose is to have a loving relationship with God, to bring glory to Him and to be a testimony to the world. Once we make up our minds to surrender our lives to Him, then we will find the peace and satisfaction that we so much deserve.

Introduction

I have met so many people who have shared with me the plans they are making to live life to the fullest. As I listened to each of them, I was sure that their intentions were good. Like me, they were probably told to work hard, do right by others, and good things would happen to them. Even with that, there's still a certain feeling inside of you saying, "Good is not good enough." As time goes on, you still feel like a restless wanderer, as if you were put here on earth to accomplish something, but you don't know quite what it is. You recognize that something is keeping you from filling that tremendous void in your life. You've got money in the bank, a degree, a nice job, the means to fly off to anywhere in the world, etc.; yet there's still something missing.

We all have good intentions, but a lot of times we either lose hope because of the burden of obstacles and unexpected setbacks, or we get comfortable, which can be dangerous.

Life Is Always in Progress...So Take the Brakes Off will give you insight into some things that you can do yourself that will put you in a position to be blessed by God and live the life that you've always dreamed about. Most suggestions shared by the author are coupled with everyday personal experiences that have followed her from childhood to adult, but with a twist and a bit of humor.

This is not a "get rich" manual—it's better than that! This book shows you how to enrich your life and enjoy all of the wonderful riches that God has in store for you, and the greatest of those riches is love and peace. When you have those two things in place, everything else will come together. Yes, when you fill that void, ideas will come from every direction in your life, and you will get just what you deserve. A lot of people feel that getting what we deserve is always negative, but listen to what I am saying here. When you do good deeds and try your best to please God and not man, He will give you what you deserve. That's when your true treasures will show up, and God will show out. He will make you an example, and the only thing you will be able to do will be to stand back and give Him the glory.

Yes, God is rich, and He will give you just what you deserve even when men think that you're undeserving. He'll give you birds to sing to you instead of hip-hop to listen to; He'll give you people to serve instead of giving you servants; He'll give you the stars to light up your property instead of security lights; He'll give you flower bouquets to pick from your very own garden instead of roses from a florist; He'll give you brooks and creeks to wade in instead of a man-made pool; He'll help you grow natural food instead of having to go to the grocery store; and He'll surround you with good neighbors instead of enclosing you with burglar bars. Our God is a rich God and wants us to share His blessings. Yes, you can have your cake and eat it, too, and you deserve just that; so sit back and let God serve it up! Think about what Louis "Studs" Terkel, an American author, historian, actor, and broadcaster, said: "I think most of us are looking for a calling, not a job. Most of us, like the assembly line worker, have jobs that are too small for our spirit. Jobs are not big enough for people."

    Once you realize that the Greater One is in you, you will not only move forward, but you will demand everything that Satan and your bad choices have taken from your life, and God will make you an overnight success. Life is always in progress, but if you want to move through life with purpose and determination, you've got to take the brakes off!

Chapter 1

Where Memories Were Made

"Before I formed thee in the belly, I knew thee… and I ordained thee a prophet (my spokesperson) unto the nations."
~~Jeremiah 1:5

My childhood memories go back to sitting outside my grandmama's house on the side porch in Sparks, Georgia. Even as a child, at the early age of two or three years old, I vividly remember the many times that I spent on those side steps. To be exact, there were three steps in a semi-circle, and they were so beautiful. Since I was young, the porch appeared somewhat like a stage to me. I remember being at my grandmother's house for a couple of years without my mother. When I got old enough to inquire about it, my mother told me that I had to go stay with Grandmama for a couple of years because she (my mother) had come down with polio immediately after I was born. As I was writing this book, I talked to my aunt Lil and my sister Eunice to see if they could give me a little more insight on dates and other background. What we determined is that my mother was either carrying me in her womb during the time that she had the virus or she came down with the virus shortly thereafter. We came to that conclusion because Eunice remembers Mama becoming ill when she turned eleven-years-old, and Eunice is eleven years older than I am. Either way, God had plans that turned out for the good for both Mama and me. In researching the polio virus on the Internet, I found that many pregnant women do not live through this type of virus. I also learned that it is contagious, and, that being true, I (or any of my siblings for that matter) could have caught the virus from Mama. Praise God that He didn't let it be so! To God be the glory!

As a child, I was a dreamer, and most days, I'd sit on those side steps with the sun rays touching my body, looking at the butterflies, bees, chickens, cats, and people walk by on the dirt roads until it was time to eat, take a bath and go to bed. I don't recall much interaction with other children or grown folks, but what I do recall was the feeling that I was loved and safe and that everything was going to be okay.

I really don't know when Mama came to get me, but I do remember that I grew up as a child on 746 Pelham Street, and I always remember Mama with a slight case of paralysis. Since I'd never seen her any other way, that was the norm for me. One thing that I know for sure is that I took after my mother. She was creative, and she always had something going on. She sewed, went to school, attended church, helped neighbors, sold Avon, was a substitute teacher at my elementary school, went on to get her degree and did hair professionally. This lady did everything and even had dinner on the table for us every night, and they weren't store-bought meals either! We had meals with meatloaf, fried chicken, pork chops, greens with ham hocks, fish, rice and gravy, cabbage, and much more; and she provided all of that without a whole lot of money. I sort of remember something like twenty dollars a week that my dad gave her for groceries. A lot of times, we had leftovers, but the food back then was much better than it is today, and we didn't mind those leftovers. Whatever the situation, Mama worked it out. Even after everything she did, she'd do our hair if needed, give baths and help with homework.

I have a lot of memories from back then. I remember my sister Pat teaching me how to count money and drive when I was older. I also remember Shirley and Eunice doing some of the cooking and watching over Pat and me while Mama was at work.

I also remember Mama telling me the story about how she ended up moving to Atlanta from Sparks, Georgia. She said that during those days, back in the 1940's, black people could only receive an education up to the eleventh grade. Since they could not receive a diploma, they could not get a decent paying job to support themselves. She said that she had a choice of either staying in Sparks and picking cotton or trying to better herself by getting an education. She chose the latter.

When she got to Atlanta, she went to beauty school and became a professional stylist, married John Henry and was doing okay until she came down with polio. Again, Mama had a choice of taking on the "poor me" mentality or trying to better herself. She heard that the federal government was giving out grants for handicapped victims, and she applied. Mama finished school with a Master's degree and taught at the elementary level until she retired.

Life is always in progress...so take the breaks off

Mama always insisted on all of us getting an education, but getting an education herself was not always easy for her. She would sometimes tell us the story about how she wore one pair of shoes the entire school year until they were so worn out that she couldn't wear them anymore. That was really funny to my daddy. I really didn't understand why he would laugh and make fun of her instead of being more supportive as she struggled to get her education. Not only did he tease my mom about her shoes, but he made it so that at times, she would actually have to sneak in the wee hours of the night in order to study. Sometimes he would walk in on her doing her homework and tear every single book up, and she would be left there crying. Still, she kept going and accomplished her goal.

My mother was determined that we would get an education and make good grades, but one thing that really bothered me about her was that she would not do my homework for me. That's how children think, and I was a typical child. Every night, we'd go through the same routine. She'd tell me to stop playing around, pay attention, make necessary corrections on my work, and hurry up because she had something else to do. I'd be crying most of the time because, to me, it was so simple for her to do it and get it over with, but she wouldn't. As I look back over my life, I appreciate her strength, and I have always thanked God that she was determined to teach her children what they needed so they would have a better life.

Besides doing our own homework, another thing we had to do was what Mama called "general cleaning," and this was on every Saturday. We did this whether we liked it or not. It felt like child abuse to the third degree! Saturday mornings, all of us had our separate chores, and we knew that there were no excuses for not getting our work done. We didn't have a lot of children's rights like there are now. To top it off, we had to go grocery shopping, get our hair done for Sunday, iron our clothes, polish our shoes and be on time for Sunday school the next morning. I remember on many Saturdays being tired and weak from spraying the cleaning chemicals. Because the FDA reports on hazardous chemicals were not advertised like they are now, we were not as knowledgeable of the harmful effects of mixing certain chemicals. Every Saturday, I would become ill after using the bleach and Clorox powder in the tub, but I had no idea what was going on and neither did Mama. I know now that the combination of those two cleaning products can be toxic. Thank God for natural products today!

Regardless of how I felt at the time, I know that every experience that I have had in my life, both good and bad, has made me the person that I am today. And yes, I love myself exactly the way my experiences allowed me to turn out. When asked if I had the chance to live my life over, would I do it differently, the answer is a definitive "No!" All of my personal experiences that came from both my parents taught me about honesty and integrity and gave me my belief in a higher power. The biggest lesson was about the power of prayer.

We as a family had some hard times and, like my mother, I prayed a lot, too—and I do mean a lot! I knew deep down in my heart that God had something planned out in my life that was especially for me. Even now, I have this unbelievable joy deep down inside that there are better days ahead. There were some hard times in the past, but God always made a way out of no way.

Despite our hard times, we were a good family. It seemed like the whole neighborhood was proud of the Hunter children. There were five of us, four girls and one boy, and we were decent kids. We weren't wild, and we all got along well with adults and the other children in the neighborhood. The teachers and our classmates liked us, the principal knew us, and our grades were good. We were in Sunday school and church every Sunday, and we were always obedient to authority. Since Mama sewed, we always dressed nicely, especially on Sundays.

We all got scholarships to college. My oldest sister Eunice was the class valedictorian and went away to Knoxville College, majoring in Chemistry. She was later featured in *Time, Fortune, Newsweek* and *Forbes 500* magazines as one of the "100 Most Industrious Minds in America's Classrooms Today." She taught chemistry and is now retired. Shirley went to Morris Brown College, became the head majorette, and received her degree in elementary education. She retired as an assistant principal and is now known as "Dr. Shirley." She's now working as a certified Christian counselor and motivational speaker and is a teacher at Clayton State University. Pat went off to Tennessee State to join the Tigerbelles (a nationally known African-American track team known for turning out more Olympians than any other college team in the country) and later became a principal.

A couple of years after Pat, I went off to Tennessee State to join the Tigerbelles and retired from education in

2004 as an assistant principal. I then started my second career with my gift basket company, Simply Blessed Gift Creations. I am now a motivational speaker and a published author in hopes of one day being on the bestseller list (with your help, of course).

My brother Vincent is a successful entrepreneur in his own right with a flourishing cleaning company. Vincent called me one Mother's Day to wish me well, and we began to talk about our childhood and our hopes and dreams for the future. As we were talking, Vincent mentioned that he had wanted to go to school to pursue a degree in counseling. When he wanted to do that as a child, Mama suggested that he take up a trade instead. I told him that Mama told me that story and that, in retrospect, she didn't feel good about it. I shared with him that she did have some regrets about not being able to put in time with him for homework and other school activities like she did with us because she was the sole provider at that time.

In listening to him, I thought, "Maybe if Mama had suggested I take up a trade instead of going off to college, I'd be living in one of the richest sections of town with two Mercedes Benzes parked in my driveway like Vincent!" Isn't that funny? Everybody seems to always want what the other person has. Like someone said, "We do not have a choice over the hand dealt us in life, but we do have a lot of control over how this hand is played." My siblings and I took control of the "hand dealt us."

Poet Maya Angelou says, "People see your glory, but they don't know your story." That is so true of our family. We looked good on the surface, but we had some tough times because our dad was an abuser. He would drink and keep the whole family up all night, fussin', cussin', pulling out his gun, and fighting. One time I saw him sitting with a gun in his hand just crying his eyes out, and I felt sorry for him. I asked him what was wrong, and he told me a little about his childhood. He kept hitting on his leg and crying. Later on, Mama told me that when he was a little boy, he got some glass stuck in his foot and it became infected. He kept begging his mother to take him to the hospital, but she wouldn't. When the infection got to the point where he had to go to the hospital, the doctors had to amputate his leg. The loss of his leg deeply affected him and probably led to his abusiveness.

Sometimes we need to look at what may be causing a people to behave like they do. I'm not suggesting that you allow people who have had negative experiences to run over you, but a lot of times, we forget that they need our compassion and prayers. The dreadful harm that we do is to allow them to make us hate them, and that, alone, gives Satan the power to run rampant and cause havoc in our lives. My daddy's actions were horrible. I have seen my mother bleed due to injuries my father inflicted, run for her life, have food thrown in her face and have a gun pulled on her.

Despite all of that, though, I still love both of my parents dearly. Satan's plot was to get to me, through my daddy's behavior, to be filled with anger and hatred, but by the grace of God, it did not work. I love my father just as if he had been the most perfect dad in the world. A lot of times I listen to Luther Vandross's song, "Dance with my Father," and pretend that it is my song between me, my mom and my dad. Although I shed tears, they are tears of joy for allowing God to remove the past from my heart and memory so that I can move on.

I would say that my dad was an alcoholic, but again, that's something that the FDA didn't begin to recognize or advertise until years later, so alcoholism never crossed my mind. In my neighborhood, there was a liquor house on the corner, and in looking back, the whole neighborhood may have been full of alcoholics! To be truthful, sometimes it was liquor that provided us with entertainment.

For example, I remember one of the biggest jokes in the neighborhood was that this little old man would get drunk, and when he'd pass by our house, he'd say what he was going to do to his wife when he got home. A lot of bleep bleeps... They lived in what the neighbors called "the big red house." The house was on the corner and right across the street from us. When the other kids and I saw him heading home and knew that he was drunk, we'd get close enough to hear what he was saying to his friend. He'd say, "Man, if my old lady don't have my dinner ready, I'm going to ^&**^*#$." The other man would be agreeing with him and egging him on all of the way until they reached his house, then they'd go their separate ways.

This man was really skinny, and the wife was very strong and hefty. I'd always wonder why his two girls, who were there with us hearing their dad talk like that, wouldn't run in the house and try to stop him from fighting their mother because here is what always happened. Just as surely as that man entered the door, he'd go rolling down the steps within a few seconds and everybody would be laughing at him. Then, when we would see him the next day with a cast on his arm, we'd ask him, "What happened to you?" or "What are you going to do if your wife doesn't have your dinner ready for you today?" He'd say the same thing, and he'd go tumbling down the steps again. That was the neighborhood entertainment, and we got more than our money's worth!

However, my family was not as fortunate as far as our mother was concerned. I can remember the times when my father was drinking that I was so scared that I don't think hell itself could have been any worse. Seriously! My dad was a hurting man, and hurting people hurt people. I know now how the spirit world operates, and I realize that Satan tried to use my dad in order to destroy an entire generation. But he wasn't successful.

That's why we have got to learn to love and forgive. I told my mama that years ago because that is what I have always believed in my heart. Yes, my father was a hurting man that took a lot of anger out on his family, but my mother was a woman that kept our family together with the help of God. I know that, unlike our family, many good lives have been destroyed because of situations like ours. If you were unfortunate enough to be in a similar situation, it is my prayer that you continue to ask God to come into your heart and remove all of the hurt and pain. You've got to keep moving, and this is something that you cannot do alone. If you are still breathing, God is waiting to help you, but only if you will allow Him. I hope that you will always remember this one thing: Everything that will happen in your life will either kill you or make you stronger. If you are reading this book, then you are still alive, and God wants you to move on with the good things that He has in store for you.

I am just thankful that God kept His hand on me and allowed grace and mercy to follow me throughout my life. We had some difficult days back then, but even when I wasn't really aware of what was going on in my life, Jesus was going before the throne constantly on my behalf pleading my case before God. So many of us take life for granted. It's a blessing to wake up in the morning because there are so many people who will not. As the Holy Spirit is guiding me on this project, He so graciously gave me a testimony to share with you about not taking life for granted (which I will discuss in more detail later). At the end of this and each chapter will be the suggestions which will position you to trust God and enjoy life for many years to come.

Count Your Blessings

There is a family of geese that live down by my pond. Five new geese were hatched about four weeks ago as of the time of this writing. While the mother sat on the nest, the father, whom I named Oscar, would not let anything or anybody go near that nest. Oscar would chase me, my grandson Tarance, my llamas and my cat if it appeared that we were headed in the direction of the nest. He protected his family with his life. Even now, the geese come up from the pond every morning to be fed, and although I feed them very well, if I get too close, Oscar makes a hissing sound to scare me off. Here's the point. Regardless of how protective Oscar was towards his family, on one particular morning when they came up to eat, one of the babies was missing; it did not make it to the pond with the rest of the family. My heart broke, tears welled up in my eyes and God told me to share this story with my readers because what happened to the goose could very well have happened to one of you—that is, it could have been you who didn't make it this morning. Something to think about, huh?!

Despite our parents' best efforts to protect us from all harm and danger, some of us have not had a good life. Nevertheless, God has kept us here although there are some people who didn't make it. None of us are guaranteed to make it. God has kept us here for a reason, yet with all of the things that God does for us, we still take life for granted. Go look in the mirror and count your blessings. Stop blaming your parents and your environment for your inertia and lack of progress. Stop complaining about your life and how your past has affected your life. Keep your mind focused only on the God who created and sustained you for a time such as this.

As I look back over my childhood, we were just a phone call away from a foster home or the Department of Family and Children Services (DFACS), but by the grace of God and a praying mother, we made it. The only reason that I'm sharing my experiences is that I know some of you reading this book are stuck on the road of hurt, shame, regret and unforgiveness, and I hope that my testimony and the story about the geese will give you something to think about. As I have said before, there are so many people who did not make it, even when their mothers or fathers did everything in their power to keep them from harm. While the love of parents is enormous, there is no greater love than the love that our Heavenly Father has for us. If Satan can continue to make you look back and wish that your life had been different, then you will not be able to move forward. God wants your progress to be for the uplifting of His Kingdom, and in order to move on, you need to take the brakes off, forgive and count your blessings.

Hardships Make You Stronger

Somewhere I heard, "If you're going through hell, keep going," and that's what Mama did. Mama was born June 19, 1927, and her birthstone is a pearl. My description of her and the things in life that she went through to make a better life for herself and her children can be compared to the story in the book *The Making of a Pearl* by Louise Powell.

History tells us that before gold was purified or diamonds cut, pearls were prized as gems of natural beauty. Ancient Romans thought pearls were the crystallized tears of angels. And even today, pearls are still admired for their soft, rich glow and are symbols of purity, harmony and humility.

Natural pearls are gems created by an accident of nature, unlike most gems which are minerals mined from under the earth's surface. After much research, scientists have concluded that when a foreign particle enters the body of an oyster or is lodged there, it is irritating to the oyster, which, in an effort to soothe the irritation, secrets layer after layer of a beautiful milky substance called nacre, mother of pearl, which covers the irritant. Most scientists agree that it is not the result of healthy conditions but stress that causes oysters to grow pearls. They have observed that many of the large beautiful, flawless pearls are found in shells which are imperfect in form or growth. Most natural marine pearl oysters are found not in placid, calm waters, but in water channels where there is a strong current. As we look at the making of a pearl, we see that great and beautiful things can blossom out of the cruelest situations.

My mother was not perfect, but God is not looking for perfect vessels to carry out His mission, and that's what Mama did. What God is looking for are people who will take Him at His Word and be willing to accept the irritant that may cause discomfort or pain. We know that God is a God of love, and His intention is not to hurt us. However, due to the unpleasant, even harsh conditions of the world, He will allow us to have certain experiences in our lives to shape and mold us into what He wants us to become. Thus, we need to embrace the lessons our hardships impart so that we can become better servants of the Kingdom and better able to deal with the challenges that lie ahead. So take the brakes off and know that hardships make you stronger.

God Answer Prayers

As I mentioned before, my mother was a praying woman. She prayed over everything, including a glass of water. Seeing my mother pray taught me how to pray. I was amazed that my very first serious prayer where my requests were actually manifested occurred when I was in the fourth grade. Not only was I amazed at the prayer being answered, but I was equally amazed at the prayer request itself. Our class had been assigned a project for Black History Week, and this assignment was to role-play a famous African-American. I chose Harriet Tubman, and I was determined to play my part to the hilt because the grand prize for the best performance was a shiny fifty-cent piece that the teacher actually showed us during class. Besides that fifty-cent piece, my other motivation was to give my grand prize to another student. What was I thinking, Lord? Whatever it was, that period of my life awakened me to the fact that I could have whatever I professed with my mouth; all I needed to do was have faith.

    It also changed my life forever, so much so that I can remember the classroom location and the desk where I sat when I presented my homework assignment. We had exactly one week to practice before the assignment was to be presented. Every morning, I would wake up and glance out of the window and pray to God that I would win. I promised God that if I won, I would give my money to a boy named Winston so that he could experience a hot meal in the cafeteria. As the days went on, I was obsessed with that fifty cents and Winston. I would come home, sit in the window and pray really, really hard and ask God if He would just let me win. Even though I was a child, I felt desperate, almost like my life depended on it. That was a strange, pure, genuine feeling for me, and I did not know where it was coming from because back then, I needed the money far more than Winston did.

    I knew that I wanted to give the money to Winston, but still I was a bit confused because I kept thinking about what I could do with the money myself, like buy a Burger

King Whopper for fifty cents, purchase two-for-a-penny cookies, or maybe even give it to Mama to help out around the house. Again, I don't really know what I was thinking because Winston seemed to be okay, and I, being somewhat of a tomboy and too young to even think about having a boyfriend, was not trying to win his affection. I knew Winston was well dressed and very studious and brought his neatly packaged, well balanced lunch to school every day, and here I was barely making it, but I still wanted that money for him! I guess it was because when lunchtime came and we all went to the cafeteria, Winston would walk into the cafeteria, sit quietly all by himself, and eat his lunch alone.

We kids who ate the school lunch seemed to have just a little more excitement and fun during that period of the school day because we all sat side-by-side and talked a little, and I wanted Winston to experience that same joy. Although I really needed the money, I just wanted to be able to put a smile on someone else's face. When I won, I gave my fifty cents to Winston, and he ate lunch with us. I was the happiest child in the universe because Winston was at our table laughing and talking with us. No one but God ever knew to this day how much I sat by that window, day in and day out, praying to win just so I could see Winston smile. God placed so much happiness on the inside of me when Winston became a part of our group. I never told my teacher, parents, or any of my classmates about this incident, but it changed my life forever.

Now I realize that this was not about wanting to see Winston smile. It was God using Winston to shape my attitude towards giving and helping. Now, I can assure everyone that you cannot escape the blessings of God when you are genuinely concerned about others. There's a saying that you can never help another person without actually helping yourself, and it is also confirmed in scripture that says it is better to give than to receive. What we don't realize is that God is setting us up to be blessed. God let me know at an early age that when you put others before yourself, He will be your Sustainer.

When we do for others, when we give our time, a portion of our income to help with Kingdom building, or any act of kindness, we need to get ready to be blessed—especially when it's a random act of kindness, and the receiver never knows about it. See, you don't always have to toot your own horn. Just allow the Holy Spirit to come in, and you will be exalted beyond belief. If we are to be good stewards of our Father, our mission is to be concerned for our fellowmen. So take the brakes off and realize that God will answer prayers.

The Secret Place

Every man, woman, boy or girl should remember the first time he or she met God and should have discovered a special place to meet with Him. I am not talking about in church, when you are all dressed up and all eyes are on you. No, I mean where you <u>really</u> meet Him—where you come face-to-face with Him, and He speaks to your quiet soul while you listen as if your life depends on what's being said. It is in this place of silence that He whispers in your ear, kisses your cheek, and stops your flowing tears. Or better yet, it's where He allows you to open up with dance, praise and tears of joy. It's almost like you're being purged and prepared for greater things in life, yet nobody knows but the two of you. It's like a secret, your secret. It's your personal meeting place where you and you alone will go and know for sure that God will meet you there. People who know me, I mean really know me, know that my meeting place is any window. It does not matter what window or what framework holds the window. It just has to be a window. That's where I speak to my God, and He meets me there every time. I encourage you to find your own secret place and draw closer to Him.

Even though I was a child when I sat in the window wishing to win the prize so I could give it to Winston, I knew what God showed me that day meant that whatever I prayed for in my life, I could get. This is true for us all—whether it's your health, relationships, children, spouse, career, finances, and just about anything else that you can imagine. If you don't do anything else for the remainder of the day, you need to put it in your heart to be determined to find that meeting spot with God and make your requests known to Him.

So how do you know when you find the right meeting place? Believe me, you'll know. You have got to want that place more than anything else in the world. Once you find a place where you can commune with the Holy Spirit, your life will change forever.

As I said earlier, my ideal spot is any window, but it has not always been a window. When I was a little girl at Grandmama's house, it was the side steps. I was so young that I could not read or write, but I felt the presence of God there. As I became older and was thrust into the workforce, my secret meeting place became my office restroom where I spent no less than 30 minutes every morning on my knees before going into the gym to teach my classes. I've never had a problem with the government taking prayer out of the classroom because I don't believe that we should be forced into worship. God loves us so much that we should enter into worship and prayer with a thankful spirit and a sense of gratitude, not because we have to, but because we want to, and that is what I did in the secrecy of my office on a daily basis. So take the brakes off and find that secret place.

You've Gotta Know for Yourself

I will never put my relationship with God in a box because He is too awesome for that. I came to that conclusion years ago when I got up one morning and was preparing for Sunday School. A pastor came on TV and asked this question, "How do you really know that there is a God? We're not talking about getting dressed up, going to church and acting like Christians. I mean, how do you know for sure that there is really a higher power?" Hearing that question was when I began to be more observant of scriptures and compared the Word of God to what was going on around me. I have no doubt that there's a God, and you shouldn't either. Just look at your life as you study the Word for yourself. I didn't say look at your life while you listen to the preacher, sing in the choir, work on the pastor's aid committee, work on the usher board, feed the hungry, or sit on the deacons' or mothers' board. I said look at your life as you study the scriptures for yourself.

Just take a look at the Word as inspired by the Holy Spirit and judge for yourself.

When you're at the end of your rope and feel there's nobody who loves you, do you know that there's a God who gave His only begotten Son for you? In this upside down economy where all of your life savings may have disappeared overnight, do you still believe that there's a God who has the master economic plan? What about the children you raised who are now too busy to pick up the phone to check up on you? Do you still know that there's a God who will never leave your side?

What about when you make a mistake that could change the entire course of your life? Guess what? He's omniscient (i.e., all-knowing), and He already knew before you made decisions—and sometimes mistakes—what choices you'd make; it didn't catch Him by surprise. He can still use you and your mistake as part of His plan. What I am saying is that even when life seems to be too much or God doesn't seem to be there, He is there and has always been there. He promised in His Word that He would never leave you or forsake you. We just have to believe Him and take him at His Word.

God's grace has followed me throughout my life, and I thank Him for allowing me to have early experiences that have solidified my faith. Like many of us, I just need to make a decision to use every fiber of my being to be the best person in life that I can be. So take the brakes off and know for yourself.

Knock and the Door Shall Be Opened

When I was in the fifth grade, I was sitting on the sofa looking at cartoons. My favorite cartoon was Hercules because it gave me a false sense of physical power. I knew that I could not actually pick up big rocks like Hercules, but seeing him do it created in me a strong spirit, determination and desire to do better.

On one particular day, Mama was in the kitchen cooking dinner, and there came a knock at the front door. When Mama opened the door, an encyclopedia salesman asked if she wanted to buy a set of encyclopedias. At the time they were called Negro History Encyclopedias. She said that she didn't have the money, but the salesman told her that she could pay twenty dollars a month. I pleaded with her, and she finally sent me to get her pocketbook. Although we didn't have a lot, I felt that picking up Mama's pocketbook was a big deal for me. It appeared that she could make things happen because she always did.

While I was sitting and watching her, she filled out the contract; the salesman then left the encyclopedias and a little bookstand. Mama went back to cooking dinner, and as I turned the pages through the encyclopedias, I saw a tall female athlete standing on the Olympic stand and her coach, Ed Temple was standing next to her. Her name was Wilma Rudolph, and what caught my interest was that she had won three gold medals in the Olympics and had overcome her condition with polio. Man, that shook me to the core because, as I mentioned before, my mom had polio. I ran to my mama, showed her the picture and promised myself that I was going to meet Wilma Rudolph one day. Little did I know that, before I was born, God had already planned our meeting in my future.

The very next day, our Physical Education teacher announced that he was going to start a track team. Because I'd always loved running, I was very excited; it was like a dream come true. I joined the team, and even though we were elementary school age, we had to compete against high school kids during the summer in order for us to get the competition that we needed, so we were running high school track times long before we went off to high school.

I remember my first state track meet at Lakewood Stadium. When I was in the ninth grade, I won the 100 yard dash, and Coach Ed Temple came up to me as I was taking off my track shoes and offered me an opportunity to run with his summer program at Tennessee State University (TSU). My question to him was, "Will you buy me a hot dog and a drink?" He did, and that made me very happy. It was only then, after the excitement of it all, that I realized that my dream had come to fruition. My summers were hard, but at least track got me off of the streets, and that made a big difference in how my life ended up.

From the time I was in elementary school, I was never allowed a single day on the streets with a lot of idle time on my hands; there was always practice with my coaches, who were Mr. Carlton, Mr. Turner, Ms. Ball and at TSU, the legendary Coach Ed Temple. Eventually, I achieved that goal I'd set when I first saw Wilma Rudolph in the encyclopedia; I thank God for allowing me the opportunity to meet Ms. Rudolph. I also had the opportunity to train under some of the best track coaches and meet some of the best athletes in the world.

When I tell that story, not only am I thankful for the fact that God saw enough in me, like He does with all of us, but also that He ordered my steps in a life-changing way. I've also told this story to share with everyone the awesome power of knowledge. Again, knowledge is POWER. Just the simple act of picking up that encyclopedia and reading it when I was in the fifth grade changed the course of my life. Never underestimate the power of education. The more you know, the farther you will go. It does not mean that you have to have a formal education; however, whatever you do in life, study your area and see how much your life will expand. Plenty of our millionaires were self-taught, but they had the ambition and thirst for knowledge.

If I had not read about Wilma Rudolph and Coach Ed Temple on that particular day so many years ago, I would have gone to a different school and missed out on a major part of history in the making. I remember one coach offering to buy me a car if I accepted the offer to attend a school in Florida, but because my motivation was meeting Wilma Rudolph, I declined the offer. Like with me, there are going to be so many opportunities knocking at your door when you align your will up with the will of God for your life. You must let God lead you to take the opportunities He means for you to have. So take the brakes off and listen for the knock of opportunity.

God Has a Plan for You

God has a strategic plan for our lives, and we cannot get around it. Around the same time in my life when I was running high school track, I met a guy that eventually became my husband. Back in those days, the school used the football players as hall monitors and for anything else that was needed around the school. I remember one day being dismissed to go to the restroom. As I was walking down the hall and getting ready to go through the double doors, the monitor, Thomas, put his arm up and told me that I couldn't pass without a hall pass. I kicked him in the shin and ran, forgetting that I had to come back that way. When I came back he said, "I like you; you're my little sister," and we started speaking to each other. We eventually started what people called "going together."

Every day after practice, we would sit under a tree and talk about the daughter that we would one day have, and all through high school, we said that her name would be Thomasita. However, years later after we married, when that day finally came that our daughter was born, we ended up naming her Terra. Our having a daughter led me to believe that you can have anything that you put your heart to.

Those early years passed, some good, some not so good, but again, everything that has happened in my life has all worked together for the glory of God. Since those days, I've moved forward with my life, and as I think back, time was going to move on even if I didn't. Times have changed since I was born in 1953, and so have I. If things stayed the same, there wouldn't be any progress. Think about it: during 1953, Queen Elizabeth II was crowned in England, Joseph Stalin died of a stroke at age 73, Dwight Eisenhower was sworn in as 34th U.S. President; and John Kennedy and Jacqueline Bouvier were wed. The Salk polio vaccine was used successfully, and the Small Business Administration was created. The average income was $4,011, a new car was $1,651, and a new house was $9,525. A loaf of bread was 16 cents, a gallon of gas was 20 cents, a gallon of milk was 94 cents, and an ounce of gold was $35. The minimum wage was 75 cents, and life expectancy was 68.2 years.

Yes, those were the "good old days," or so they say, but I am glad that I am here to see this day, today, and I thank God for all of the changes which have taken place.

Do you know that this is a great day to be alive? God is pouring out His blessings today like at no other time in history, so take the brakes off and discover how to live life more abundantly!

Chapter 2

You've Gotta Show Up

"Oh, that you would bless me and enlarge my territory!"
~~1 Chronicles 4:10 (NIV)

Let's begin by looking at auto racing soon after the construction of the first successful gas-fueled automobiles. Before that time, horse drawn buggies were used for competition and entertainment, but as we all know, progress waits on no one. The first race car contest was organized by Monsieur Fossier, Chief Editor of Paris publication *Le Vélocipède*. The winner of this contest was a man by the name of Georges Bouton, a French engineer. Why did Bouton win on that bright sunny day? It's simple. He won the race because he was the only one to show up!

Although one of the biggest blessings and real riches is that of contentment and peace, most of us want more more power, more popularity and more wealth. For most of us, it's really hard to imagine going through this life being fully content and at peace with what we have—we just want more, more, more. I am not saying that wanting God to enlarge your territory is a bad thing; however, I am saying that there is more to life than possessions. If you want to live out your full potential, you have got to have other goals, then put forth a certain amount of effort to make it possible to achieve your goals.

If you're at a point in your life, where you're feeling defeated, discouraged or unfulfilled, where you're not satisfied with what you've accomplished, or you know that you need to do something else, this may be a good time to sit back and evaluate why you are in the same position that you were in ten years ago. Every waking moment should be a new day and a new experience for the good of God's Kingdom. At some point, we need to make a commitment to move on with our lives. Stop saying, "One day I'll get to it" or "I wish I could" or "I should have." If we are to move ahead, we need to recognize that each and every day is going to come and go whether we are involved or not. The point when we become uncomfortable with our present situation is the point where we know that God is doing a new work in our lives. No more excuses. Thomas Edison said, "Discontent is the first necessity to progress."

God has special plans for you. He knew you before you were born and every moment was laid out before your physical presence became a reality on this earth. I strongly believe that nothing happens by accident.

God wants us to be Kingdom builders, but how can we do that if we don't have anything to offer? If we profess to be blessed, then our walk should reflect a life of progress and not that of someone with a victim mentality. We should not be afraid to go forward and see what God has in store for us. I am not specifically talking about having money; rather, I am talking about enjoying simple pleasures and having a life full of peace and happiness with your family and friends—and having a feeling of accomplishment and purpose.

There are plenty of things that may be holding you back, and some may never come to your mind unless you pray and ask God to reveal them to you. I know that this may sound elementary, but I want to share something from my childhood that made me feel that I was unworthy of receiving God's best for my life. Believe it or not, one thing that had me in bondage for quite some time was the songs that we sang in church. Some of them seemed depressing and made me feel there was no hope or that I was doomed. Others just plain scared me! There were so many times when those songs made me question my future and my relationship with God. I remember songs like "I'm running, trying to make a hundred, 'cause ninety-nine and a half just won't do."

As a child, I knew that one hundred percent was a lot, so that counted me out, especially when I looked at my report card which revealed that I was really far from one hundred! Another song was "Swing low, sweet chariot, coming for to carry me home." All I could think of was a big chariot coming out of the sky, and I pictured a man with a whip chasing me. I thought like that because the only chariot that I'd ever seen was in the cartoon Hercules. I didn't know how a whip felt, but I knew how an extension cord and a switch felt, as I had gotten my share of both. Then there were songs like, "I'm ready to go home to be with the King." Again, when I saw a king on television, he was mean and unapproachable, so the idea of going to live with a king was kind of scary. The song that really got to me, though, was the one that included, "I'm tired and weak, and I just want to go home and be with the Lord." I remember thinking, "I hope God knows that this is just a song because I haven't been on earth that long, and I've got plenty of energy! I'm not ready to leave here yet!"

Although I saw and heard some things that I did not understand as a child, there were some things that I have never forgotten. I remember seeing the deacons on their knees for what appeared to be hours, moaning and groaning, and those experiences have never left me. It's in those experiences that I discovered my strength, for I learned that it's through ardent prayer that I can meet my God; it's in my communion with Him that my prayers are answered. My memories of those deacons are precious to me, and I thank God for allowing Mama to raise us in church. When I was a child, I thought as a child, but now, I understand. Those learning experiences occurred about fifty years ago, and I appreciate everything that God has done to bring me to this point.

As I said before, you will not make any change unless you're just sick and tired of being sick and tired. Remember, "Discontent is the first necessity to progress." That's why it's hard to make people do or be something if they are content with where they are. In order to move ahead, we have to be uncomfortable enough to confront our issues.

This chapter deals with "showing up," and when I talk about "showing up," I am basically speaking of making an attempt to make your life situation better than what it is at the present moment. You have got to have some sense of direction, and most times our examples and our direction in life come from our parent's teachings, specifically what they will and will not tolerate. We couldn't sit around Mama's house and do nothing. The rule was you either go to school or get out, and you didn't just sit around the house wasting time. Mama gave all of us responsibilities. When I was in elementary school, I can remember her calling home, telling me what items to put on for dinner because she was on her way home and wanted to get a head start. Mama's giving us responsibilites taught me that we should raise our children so that one day they will be able to go out on their own and become responsible citizens.

If we do not teach children at an early age to make an effort, they will most likely be dependent on us, i.e., their parents, and, thus, have no reason to "show up." I tried to pattern my life after my mother's teachings about being strong and standing on your own. As a result, the biggest gift that both my daughters have ever given me was the gift of their being self-sufficient. Both began working in high school and acquired the means to pay for all of the name brand fashions and extra activities they wanted; they sponsored themselves. Again, you have to take the brakes off and make your children become responsible. You will be glad you did; by doing so, you will be able to enjoy your "twilight" years as it was intended, for God promised in His Word that our latter days would be greater than our first.

Some of us have made tremendous progress towards doing what we are called to do as believers. Also, some of us have gone over and beyond in acquiring an education and financial status that would qualify us as being successful according to worldly standards.

By the same token, some are wondering why they can't seem to get ahead in life or at least break even. Could it be that there are still doors that need to be closed? There may be doors that you're not even aware of. Could it be anger, fear, distrust, laziness, pride, envy, a failure to forgive, or other negative emotions that are blocking our blessings? God has his arms opened wide to embrace you and listen to your desires. He has a wonderful plan for your life, and He does not want you to be in bondage.

Remember, God loves you and is just as excited when you call upon Him as you are when your children or grandchildren call to chat with you. Sometimes I hear ministers say, "God doesn't need us; we need Him." However, I disagree; we need each other. Our every being is dependent on Him, and He is depending on us to lead other lost souls to Him. God created man for relationships—relationships with others and a relationship with Him. But here's the catch. Although God created us for a relationship with Him, if we don't get it together and do what we're called to do, He's got other men and women to whom He will pass our blessings. If we don't want to miss our blessings, we need to take the brakes off and walk into our season.

God has so much that He wants to share with us, but we must be open to receiving it. If you're feeling that you know that you can do much more than what you're doing now, He is speaking to you. If there is something weighing on your heart and constantly tugging at you over and over again, I believe that God is trying to get your attention because there is something that He wants you to do. We've got His DNA, so we are born to be successful. Remember that it's never too late to fulfill your dreams. Success doesn't care how old you are, but like I said earlier, you've got to try. "You've gotta show up."

Successful people see themselves as being successful before they actually hold the prize. They don't just roll out of bed one day and decide "today is my day to win." Instead, they are people of faith and determination, and they keep working toward what they want. James 5:1-8 (NIV) says, "See how the farmer waits for the land to yield valuable crop and how patient he is for the autumn and spring rains." You, too, must be patient and stand firm.

Indeed, those who show up to win are not just hard workers; they also have character, patience, perseverance, and courage. In the sections that follow, I will relay some personal stories related to these attributes.

Always Tell the Truth

Sometimes, Christians overlook the little things that block their blessings. Wrong is wrong, and a lie is a lie. I absolutely hate lies with a passion! There is no need to mislead people. Some people feel that telling an untruth only is deceitful, but a deceitful spirit comes in other forms: bragging, flattery, exaggerating, sneaky behavior, siding with wrong behavior, copying other people's material (tapes, videos), not speaking up for others who are being sabotaged, or taking credit for someone else's work. What do you think of these types of behavior? Are you guilty? Sometimes we go through life and just brush these vices off, but these may be some of the things that we are not aware of that could be causing us to live unvictoriously.

A couple of months ago, Steve Harvey came out with a bestseller called *"Act Like a Lady; Think Like a Man"*, which circulated around the Internet. Can you believe that I received copies from my so-called Christian friends? Yes, but as soon as I received it, I hit my delete button. And those same people are shocked when you do or say something to them that they feel is not "Christianfied" (my word). But a sin is a sin is a sin. I need to tell the truth here. After I deleted the book, I was bored one evening, and I did try to pull it back up, but, thank God, it was gone! I didn't need to read any parts of that book, especially since I had not purchased it!

Another time, years ago, the bank accidentally gave me a $12,000 credit, and it took me a year to convince them that the money didn't belong to me. A couple of years later, I had a $42,000 room addition that was supposed to take three years to pay off. After two months of payments, the bank sent me a notice of paid in full. Again, it took a couple of months for me to convince them that they had made a mistake. In both cases, I could have profited from the world's standpoint; however, to take that money that didn't belong to me would have brought into question my Christianity.

I share these incidents to say that when you think you're getting by, you're not. Even the little things, like taking something without permission with the intention of returning it, are not acceptable. So take the brakes off; always be honest and tell the truth.

Let's Give 'Em Something to Talk About

Believers assemble to worship but sometimes represent Christ in a different fashion when they go their separate ways. We can't do that; we cannot have nonbelievers talking about all of the unchristianlike deeds we do. But they do need to talk about us. Let's give nonbelievers something to talk about as we strive to represent our Father with a heart full of gratitude and thanksgiving wherever we go, not just at church. We have the power to change the world, and there are plenty of people who are willing to follow if we get out of the middle of the road and take a stand for what is right. So take the brakes off, and make a decision today to give 'em something to talk about!

All That and a Bag of Chips

When is the last time that you've looked in the mirror and said, "How great thou art," referring to yourself? You know you're headed for destruction when you think you're "all that and a bag of chips." Remember, pride goes before the fall. Pride is one of the worst sins that one could ever imagine. Proverbs 6:16-19 puts pride at the top of the list of the things that God hates the most. In fact, He doesn't even like a proud look. Additionally, the Bible points out that pride is the sin that turned the archangel into Satan. Thomas Brooks, a Puritan preacher and author, said the following: "There is no tongue that can express, or heart that can conceive the horrid sins and miseries that pride has ushered in among the children of men."

The one quick test to see if you have that sin in your life is how you react when you're being criticized for something. If your reaction is indignation and resentment, then pride is at work in your heart. You become angry when you are criticized because your pride is hurt, and that can be the beginning of your downfall. Even if the criticisms are not true, it's your reaction on which you're being judged.

If pride has caused you to miss out on a lot of things that you think you deserve in life, it's not too late to reclaim them. Just ask God to come into your heart and help you accept the fact that this may be you. Ask Him to take away that pride. Remember, "God resists the proud but He gives grace to the humble" (James 4:6). So take the brakes off and drop the 'tude!

Be Dependable

I learned about dependability the hard way. One day I promised my grandson Tarance that I would take him to the Dollar Tree and buy him a bunch of toys. When he thought it was time to go, he came running to me all excited saying, "Mema, it's time to go." When I told him that I was tired and we would do it the next day, he was really disappointed. The look on his face reminded me of the people that I had disappointed in the past, and I didn't feel good about that. I have decided to stop making promises, but if I do make them, I am determined to keep them. So whatever you do, take the brakes off and be dependable!

Ask for What You Want

My daughter Terra went off to cheerleading camp one summer, and she was chosen by the National Cheerleading Association to represent Georgia in the Macy's Day Parade. She showed me the letter and, knowing that participating would cause a financial strain on me, said, "That's okay, don't worry about it." I don't know where she got that spirit. At the time, she was working at McDonald's. You know she was not making much money, so I made an appointment to see the owner, Mack. Since she had only been there for two months, I thought I would ask him for a small donation.

I intended to keep asking for donations until I raised the $1,200 that was needed for the trip. I asked Mack if he could give me a $25 donation, and after he thought about it for a while, he said that he needed to go into his office and see what he could come up with. Mack came back with his checkbook and asked me the cost of the entire trip. Again, I said it was $1,200 but I was just asking for $25. When he handed over the check, I discovered he had written it for the entire amount of the trip. A lot of people do not realize that others are ready to help if you will just ask.

Still don't believe it's that simple? I'll share another story with you. Years ago, when I first started my gift basket company, I went to network meetings where I was instructed to seek contracts by making calls and setting up appointments for those with whom I wanted to do business. That was the professional way of doing it in the business industry. However, the very first contract that I received was when Mitch walked into the gym, and I said, "Hey

Mitch, what about sending gift baskets to your clients?" From him, I got my first business contract without having to search, dress up, or go out and network. Again, it's the determination to make things happen in your life and not waiting for everything to be in place that brings success. Sometimes just going with your gut feeling is all you may need.

Yet another story is about my first job interview as a school teacher. I was very thankful and appreciative that I got hired right out of school, and I was excited about having the opportunity to have an interview with the school principal. After the interview, the principal asked, "Do you have any questions?" I said, "When can I retire?" He said that I could retire at age 52 or in 30 years. I said, "Thank God." He laughed at me and hired me anyway. I asked for 30 years, and God accelerated my retirement and gave me 29 years instead. Sometimes we are afraid to say what we really feel, or we may be too shy to ask important questions that may affect our career. Don't be! Not only do people understand that you are human, but they admire you for having the courage to ask questions. Sometimes when we are afraid to speak up, we may limit ourselves from some of the things that we most deserve in life. So take the brakes off and ask for what you want.

Don't Just Stand There, Say Something

The worst thing that a person can do is not speak up for the truth and right. How many of you choose to not get involved if it doesn't have anything to do with you? As Dr. Martin Luther King, Jr. said, "There comes a time in a person's life when silence is betrayal." Albert Einstein said, "The world is a dangerous place to live; not because of the people who are evil, but because of the people who don't do anything about it." Don't be intimidated when wrong is involved. People who are being mistreated or cheated and abused may need your help. As always, keep God in the midst because standing up for right can be pretty challenging. If we want to make a change in this world, we have got to get the courage to speak up, though. Speak up for the children, speak up for the community, and speak up for what's right. Whatever you do, speak up!

I have come across a few people who have been beating the drum for change over the past years; some have made progress while, for some, things still remain the same. Eugene T. was one of the biggest drum majors during the integration of our school system, and we see the fruits of his labor. John E. and Gil T. are still our voices for change in our community and around the county, and we see their impact. When you're silent or you're afraid to speak up because you feel that you are going to be punished, that's betrayal. There are people who put their trust in you, so you cannot remain silent. You may not always be right, but in speaking up, you're getting minds to think, and pretty soon you will come to a solution.

Speaking up is not always easy, though. When I would go up to my granddaughter Victoria's school to volunteer for field trips, I would always be greeted by the teacher telling me that Victoria had excellent conduct. The more I observed Victoria's behavior, the more I realized that she was being quiet so that she could get the smiley face stickers as a reward. One day we went on a field trip to the circus, and all of the other kids were up yelling and having a good time, but Victoria was sitting quietly like she was in the classroom, being very mannerable and trying to win the approval of the teacher. When I talked to my daughter about Victoria, we made a decision to try to change that situation. I don't know if Terra ever spoke with the teacher about stopping the praise for Victoria's silence, but the child has gotten better over the years. The point of the matter is that I did not want Victoria equating silence with good behavior. We need individuals who will speak up and speak out. When children speak out or say what's on their minds, we need to stop labeling them as being "bad." We need to teach them that speaking up is okay, and we need to let them know that there's a place and a time to speak.

A lot of adults are still having problems from their childhood because they have been told to "leave it alone"; therefore, when someone approaches them, with a concern about something they have done or some fault that they have and perhaps want an explanation, they feel intimidated and think the other person is trying to cause confusion. Many times they become defensive and argumentative when the other person may simply be trying to clear the air and get on with life because he/she cares about the relationship. Being afraid to speak up and not wanting anyone else to speak up towards you can cause many problems.

All of my life I have spoken up for what is right, regardless of who my audience is or what title they may hold. If I see someone being taken advantage of, I will not sit back and let them fight that battle alone. I hate seeing a person being mistreated or ganged up on whether I know them or not. I am always for the underdog—and you should be, too!

Sometimes, mistreatment is open and blatant; however, sometimes, the person being mistreated may not even realize it. For example, there may be a situation where people are gossiping about someone, but the victim is oblivious to what is going around the office about them. In such a situation, you may want to pull that person to the side and share (in a loving way) that they may need to check themselves because they are the subject of gossip. Also, you may be aware of situations where people are being set up. Like me, you should choose to inform them so they won't walk into the trap, especially, if they are innocent in the situation. I just can't sit back and watch people go down. Again, you may need to be careful because not everyone is receptive to help, and, upon hearing what you say, they may take their anger out on you. However, you should at least try to help. Your efforts may just be appreciated!

I certainly appreciated being pulled aside one time. Years ago, I went to a cookout, and a man came over and started talking to me. I noticed this young lady looking at me. She continued to stare, then eventually she came over to introduce herself as Shirley. We talked for a couple of minutes, and she asked me if I knew the man. The more we talked, the more I thanked God for sending her my way. She shared so much with me about the man that made me realize that I did not want to be bothered with him. By going out of her way and speaking up, Shirley probably saved me a lot of time and heartache. We are living in a time when we do need to be our brother's keeper. So take the brakes off, and don't just stand by; say something!

Help Yourself

There's a book by Dave Pelzer entitled, *"Help Yourself"*. If you have not already read Pelzer's story, please let that be your next purchase because after reading his story you will never complain again, and you will want to help yourself.

Stop looking for people to do things for you—help yourself! There are so many ways that you can make your life better. We all need help from others, but we must first look around and see what we can do for ourselves. Some people feel that if they weren't born with a silver spoon in their mouths, the world owes them, but that's not true. However, there are times when we need a little boost, but even if that's the case, remember that you can't take people for granted and make them feel obligated to help you. You are responsible for your own destiny. Listen to the words of the late, famous James Brown, "I don't want nobody to give me nothing; open up the door; I'll get it myself." Yes, help yourself and watch God show up in whatever you're trying to do.

Again, we've got to do things ourselves. Some of us are sitting around waiting to see what the new President is going to do. President Obama has his hands full, and rather than wait to see how he will help us, we need to help him. I know that Washington, DC, has come out with the stimulus package, but we've got to create ways that we can operate in our daily lives to create our own stimulus plan. There are so many ways that we can create wealth. I have known people who have started their own small business after being laid off, and now they are thankful for losing the old job because now, they will never work for anybody again. So take the brakes off and help yourself!

Make Your Own Luck

Someone once said, "For every failure, there's an alternative course of action. You just have to find it. When you come to a roadblock, take a detour." This is especially related to my daughter Thomi. Thomi ran the 100-yard dash while she was in elementary school and during the summer months. However, when she entered high school, that particular event became very competitive, and she didn't stand out. I knew that she had the speed, but I had to think of an event that needed something more than speed and at the same time would put her over the top if she mastered the technique. Being her coach, I observed that very few girls ran the hurdles and that a lot of the girls who ran hurdles did not have proper technique and could easily be beaten if they had a little competition. So I decided to change her event. That was it! I would change her event and let her sister help her. Although her sister was a big help, the more competitive the event became, the more expert coaching she received.

Over the years, that particular sport became even more competitive, and I hired Henry, who was one of the best hurdle coaches in the state of Georgia, to work with her. As a result, Thomi went on to win three state championships and received a track scholarship. If I hadn't had the initiative to make that change, Thomi would have been paying back a student loan today! So, don't settle with what life gives you. Take the brakes off and make your own luck!

Yes We Can

I really love the "Yes We Can" slogan because it shook up the entire world and brought hope to a lot of Americans. I believe that with all of my heart, and it has been one of my greatest inspirations.

Although we may not be where God wants us to be, we should continue striving each day to do our best and keep believing that "Yes We Can!" That's what this book is all about. You know that there is more to life than what you're doing, and I hope that you have made up your mind to continue the search for what God has for you. God wants you to become everything that you were meant to be. He knows the end of our story, but He also has given us choices.

Don't forget that God has specific plans for your life; if you are feeling discontent, it's that small voice of God encouraging you to go on and be the best that you can be. You can do it, and there is no greater time than right now to go for it. If you don't know where to start, start by going before God in prayer and asking Him to reveal your purpose for being here on this earth. But I hear you saying, "You just don't know how many times I've tried before." Have you tried letting go and giving it all to Him? Go ahead, take the brakes off, and know that if you can't do it, God can. Yes, we can. Yes, you can. Yes, He can—and He will!

Remember, with the right character and with courage and determination, you have what it takes to "show up" and be successful. As long as you allow the Spirit to lead you, you're going to be okay; however, you need to be aware that the moment you get it in your heart to become successful, there will be obstacles that you will have to overcome. But don't be alarmed. The overflowing power of God will overcome every obstacle in your life, and you will begin to live a life that you could only have imagined. So take the brakes off and decide today that you're going to begin to live the life He intended for you!

Chapter 3

Take Your Mark

"Therefore, my beloved brethren, be ye stedfast, unmovable [sic] always abounding in the work of the Lord, forasmuch as ye know that your labour is not in vain in the Lord."
~~1 Corinthians 15:58

This chapter and the next are best described using track and field terminology. If you've ever been to a track meet and heard the commands of the starter, you know that the first command is, "Runners, take your mark."

That is the command for the runners to step up to the starting line in preparation to compete. When that command is given, there is a hush that comes over the crowd, and all eyes are on the competitors. When they step up to the line, there's no turning back. They've each paid a price to get there, and someone else has paid a price to help them get there as well. Although they want the prize for themselves, they are equally determined to do their best because they do not want to let others down who are depending on them. Whether it is the coaches, parents, sponsors or their teammates, they just want to make their supporters proud.

Life is always in progress...so take the breaks off

I've known runners to go through all sorts of rituals at the line: taking deep breaths, jumping up and down, doing quick high-knee actions, kissing their chain and pointing to the sky or doing whatever it takes to keep them motivated and encouraged—and to the finish line before the other runners. In other words, they did whatever it took to receive the grand prize of first place.

On the command, some runners will get down on one knee while others may stand, depending on the race. As a former sprinter and a track coach, I know that getting in the starting block will give you a huge advantage over your opponent.

That's the way it is in our walk with Christ. Those who make the commitment to bow down and worship him will be the ones who will come out ahead of the game. But one thing my late husband would always say is, "You've got to focus." In order to be victorious in your life you have to stay focused on your goal and keep your eye on the prize, even when those around you are being distracted. When you're getting ready to make your mark on life and go for the gold, you cannot look to the left or the right. You can't be bothered with people that are afraid to move on, and you certainly don't have the strength to carry anybody.

It's just you and God, face-to-face. Each man must work out his own salvation. If you go around in life trying to take care of everyone else, you will never live the life that God has planned for you. You will find yourself in an unfulfilled prayer life, asking God to help you with your situation when all you've got to do is help yourself. It's only when you realize that this is not a dress rehearsal and that you only have one shot here on this earth that you will take the brakes off and release everything in life that has been holding you back.

Yes, sometimes those who are holding you back may include family or some of your running buddies, people leaning on you and depending on you to pay their way through life. Do yourself a favor, though. Cut them loose; plan a trip without having to pay anyone else's way. Go it alone for awhile. Not only will you be doing a service to those who were holding you back by making them more responsible, but you will free God up to answer more of your prayers so that you can be a blessing to the Kingdom. I guarantee you that God will give you the resources that will take you places and show you things that you've never experienced before. However, if you choose to keep hanging around the same deadbeat, no money, negative-talking people, you are going to keep feeling drained and tired, and life will most definitely pass you by. At some point in your life, you just have to make up your mind that you are going to move forward.

Look at your life now. Yes, stop what you're doing, go to the mirror and take the time to be honest with yourself, one on one. Are you where you want to be at this stage of the game? Are there some things that you've been putting off because of your busy schedule? Are you being responsible to someone who is ungrateful and doesn't have your best interest at heart? What is it exactly that's holding you back? The only way that this picture is going to change is that you change. Remember, you are only here for a season, and your obligation is to please God and not man. However, you may be surprised to find out that it's you who's holding you back. Bestselling author Napolean Hill said, "The secret of making something work in your life is, first of all, the deep desire to make it work: then the faith and belief that it can work: then to hold that clear definite vision in your consciousness and see it working out step by step, without one thought of doubt or disbelief."

As I mentioned earlier, those who bow down and worship God will be the ones that come out ahead of the game. I am not talking about church people; I am talking about anybody who submits his/her life to the Creator. Race, nationality, gender, education and being on the church roll have nothing to do with your salvation. Although God wants us to fellowship with other believers, don't think that you're going to burn in hell's fire because you do not. Let me put it this way.

If God is the head of your life and you really want a relationship with Him, you will go to a place of fellowship because you will have that insatiable urge to be around others like you. I am saying this because if you are not a member of a church, I do not want you to feel condemned. God loves you, and if you believe Him and take Him at His Word, you need only ask Him to put a feeling in your heart that will not let you rest until you find that place of fellowship.

You might be saying, "The worst people are church people," or you may have once been a member of a church where something happened that made you want no part of church ever again in your life. Bingo! Satan has you right where he wants you, alone so that he can get to you, little by little. Hosea 4:6 says, "My people are destroyed for lack of knowledge." Satan is trying to isolate you from friends and family so that when he attacks, you won't have anybody in your prayer corner. If, however, you have fostered a relationship with other Christians and those who are going in the same direction as you would like to go, you will get support from them against the devil.

Hanging around other people doing the same things that you wish to do can certainly be a blessing, especially if you have the desire and determination to get what you want. I am reminded of when my grandson Tyler celebrated his birthday at Chuck E. Cheese. As I was walking around with my granddaughter Elizabeth playing video games, Tyler walked past us, stopped and tried to make Elizabeth get up so he could sit there. He kept pushing and pushing until Elizabeth went on to another game. He got what he wanted! After sitting down and observing what was going on, he noticed the little kid sitting next to him banging on a button on a water gun which activated the gun to squirt. Tyler started banging on a gun, too. Even though he banged and banged, nothing came out of his water gun because he had not put a coin in.

When nothing happened, Tyler looked up at me, looked at the water gun, looked at the kid, and then started banging again. Again, nothing happened because he had not made the right connection to make the gun work; he needed a coin to put in the gun to make it work. After awhile, the other kid just reached in his bucket and started sharing his coins with Tyler. The moral of this story is this: If you want something badly enough, you've got to work at getting it. If you don't give up, you'll make the right connection, and you'll eventually get what you came for.

So take the brakes off and go back to church, renew your relationship with your Christian family, and be the change you want to see!

It is imperative that we keep a connection with our Christian family as well as maintain a relationship with God through sharing time with Him and staying in His Word. Read on to see how!

Believe in the Spirit World

Ephesians 6:12 says that "We wrestle not against flesh and blood, but against principalities, against powers, against the rulers of the darkness of this world, against spiritual wickedness in high places." Being aware that there is an ongoing force in the spirit world is the first step to getting on with your life. You know how some people say, "Don't take it personal?" Well, take this personally. There is an ongoing battle between good and evil, and you are the target. You are in a one-on-one battle with Satan. If you are not aware of this, you are at a great disadvantage.

Don't give Satan the advantage by thinking that he is against all believers in general. No, he wants you in particular! And don't think that all of his attention is on high profile people who make the headlines. Think again. His aim is an attack on you, so keep your guard up, knowing that the spirit world does impinge on the natural world. During the time that my son-in-law, Shawn, was training to get his pilot's license, he was involved in a motorcycle accident. I received a phone call from my daughter telling me that she was at the hospital. When I spoke with a lady who was at the scene of the accident, she said that Shawn had hit a low trailer bed that was being pulled by a truck. She said, "I was praising God, rebuking Satan and calling that boy back to life." She went on to say that she was screaming, "Satan, you can't have this one," and she was pleading the blood of Jesus and claiming Shawn's deliverance.

As she spoke with me, I could truly feel her anointing, and I pictured angels in heaven coming to the rescue. That's the kind of people that I want in my camp. If you keep on being cute, not knowing about the spirit world, you will watch Satan tear your whole household apart. Real power is pleading the blood of Jesus over your life and being bold about it. It's a really sad situation when grown people go to church week after week and do not know how to call down the "Holy Ghost Power!"

It was years before Shawn's health allowed him to pursue his dream of being a pilot, but he finally finished his training and was ready for his first interview. The day before he was to go for the interview, we had a discussion, and he shared with me that he was prepared. Shawn also said that he was comfortable because he himself had tutored someone else who had gotten hired the week before, so he (Shawn) didn't anticipate any problems.

I listened very carefully, and after Shawn finished, I shared with him that life doesn't always work out the way we think it should. See, I have been in tune with the spirit world for a long, long time and I knew that things could easily go wrong, despite his being prepared. I told him that sometimes crazy things happen. With this in mind, we went ahead and prayed together. My aunt Lil called at the very moment we were praying, and she also prayed with him over the phone.

The next day, Shawn went for his interview, and all went well as expected. However, he later called and asked me to look in my office to see if his flight book, which was his record of flight time, was near the computer because he thought that he left it at the house. I looked but found no book. I then looked over the entire house, but no luck. Shawn came to the house and searched, but again no book. He went over to his mother's house to look for it, but it wasn't there either. He went back to the airport and explained the situation, but, of course, he was not allowed to fly a $30 million plane without proof of flight time. Shawn finally came back to the house and said that he passed the interview part and that they would allow him to return on the next day to do the flight part. He was comfortable with that, especially because it gave him extra time to find the book.

He again searched the house throughout looking for the book, but to no avail. The deadline passed—and he could not be hired for the position. A couple of days later as he was looking through his briefcase, he found the book. And guess what? The book had been there all along—and it was the very same briefcase that he had taken to the interview. That's how the spirit world works, so don't take it lightly. Satan is out to destroy and embarrass you, and you must be prepared for the battle. So take the brakes off, and believe in the spirit world!

Be Alone with Him

Songwriter C. Austin Miles is so eloquent in his song "In the Garden" when he writes:

"I come to the garden alone while the dew is still on the roses,
And the voice I hear falling on my ear, the Son of God discloses.
And He walks with me and He talks with me,
And He tells me I am His own.
And the joy we share as we tarry there,
none other has ever known."

A garden is a wonderful place for seclusion, and I created what I call "Elizabeth's Garden" for that very reason. This is a place I can go sometimes when I want to be alone with God.

I need you to work with me on this one now. Sit back, relax and close your eyes. Can you think of that one special person with whom you wish you could be alone right now? The experience of the two of you just walking slowly, talking and having your sweetie whispering in your ear is wonderful. God feels the same way about you. You see, we are the apple of God's eye, and we were created to fellowship with and worship Him. He doesn't just want us to fellowship with Him; he wants us to be excited about it. The more alone time that we spend, the more direction and guidance He will give us. He gave us that promise in His Word. If you really want to know your true purpose in life, take time and listen to that still small voice. It's hard to hear it if you're always rushing, so you will have to put aside everything that will take your attention away from Him.

Everything that we have belongs to God. Our life is dependent on Him. If we don't find the time to spend with Him, situations will come up in our lives that will force us to spend that time with Him. Your prayer life should be one of gratitude and love, not for last minute emergency situations. Would you want your special person to be with you because he wants to or because he has to? Take some time for yourself, take the brakes off, and spend some alone time with God—and be excited about it!

God Is Trying to Tell You Something

Why are you feeling that your life is not complete? Why are you feeling the need to do more with your life? Why do you have the same thoughts over and over again? Maybe God is trying to tell you something. There is something that God wants you to do to help fulfill His Kingdom. If you step out on faith and trust Him, you will be surprised where your life may go.

Maybe you want to become a millionaire, but you don't have time because you're stuck in that dead-end job making money for someone else. That little thought about going back to school or taking your invention to an attorney may be just the key to your millions. Here's one thing, though. If you keep ignoring that voice, you will become immune to it and will miss out on your blessings. So take off the brakes and listen to that voice. Maybe God is trying to tell you something!

A Mind Is a Terrible Thing to Waste

There are so many brilliant minds in the graveyard. We are the richest country in the world, and with all of the opportunities and resources available to get an education here, there is no excuse for ignorance. Some people lost their lives and others sold everything they had in order to live in this land of opportunity.

A great part of education is learning God's Word. This we must do in order to please God. As stated earlier, Hosea 4:6 says, "My people are destroyed for lack of knowledge." If we really want to please our Heavenly Father, we will take the brakes off and study the Word. Remember, a mind is a terrible thing to waste.

With the desire to do things that are pleasing in the eyes of God and an honest desire to get along with our fellowmen, we are putting ourselves in a position to accomplish the many things that will make us representative of the Kingdom. Yes, this world is in desperate need of kingdom builders, and the Word teaches us how to do that. So take the brakes off and become kingdom builders!

Chapter 4

Get Set – Go

"Now set your mind and heart to seek (inquire of and require as your vital necessity) the Lord your God."
~~1 Chronicles 22:19 (AMP)

When you set out to do something, you make a decision to accomplish the project with an end in mind. You are on a mission to complete your project, whether it's in your social circle, in the business sector of your life or with your family. In doing so, you must stay focused on the finished project, and most times there is a reward at the end of the road, whether it's monetary or simply peace of mind in your accomplishment.

When we set our minds with a determination to do something, there will be obstacles that come in our path that may cause us to lose our concentration. Regardless of the situation, though, keep your mind set. Webster's definition of the word "set" is "to raise up and make ready." That is exactly what we do in track and field on the "get set" command. God is looking for a "get set, get up" spirit.

Regardless of what you're going through, keep that "get up" spirit. We get down to praise and pray to our Heavenly Father, and it's on the set position that He raises us up. If we keep our mind set on Him, we will come out victoriously!

Ralph Boston, Olympic gold medalist, has said: "Being the first to cross the finish line makes you a winner in only one phase in life. It's what you do after you cross the line that really counts." So many times those of us who have experienced past success can grow stagnate, becoming complacent with our previous wins and not pushed to keep going after the win. One thing that we as Christians need to realize is that God is involved in everything that's moving forward, going to higher levels. We must continuously motivate ourselves to reach new heights and always strive for what's better, regardless of what position you started out in, in life. Of course, God has great plans for us, but He will not force those plans on us. If we want to improve ourselves, we have got to make the commitment to make that change. As believers, this is not an easy road to travel because as soon as you attempt to make progress, the enemy will come immediately to steal your faith.

If you can believe that Christ lives in you, your direction will be easier, though. When you are tired, frustrated, and disgusted with the world, remember that you are in this world, but you are not of this world. Jesus promised in the book of John that if He is lifted up from the earth, He will draw all men unto Him. That means that when He is lifted up, you too will be lifted up, for there's no separation between Him and you; God will not allow His people to be defeated.

Look at your life. Have you ever wondered why the bad economy doesn't seem to be bothering you? Check out your bank account. Although the money may not seem to be enough to pay the bills, for some reason there is always enough. This happens when you are headed where Christ wants you to be—and that is in the direction which will bring others to Christ.

We all know that we are not immune to sin, but once we realize a disconnection, which, in essence, is a result of sin, we must make a quick decision to reconnect with the spirit of God lest we become easy targets for Satan. The Bible says in Proverbs that "A just man falleth seven times and riseth up again"; thus, the righteous know that they can't remain in sin; they must get up. So, take the brakes off and adopt a "get up" attitude that will help usher others into the Kingdom!

Following are more ways that you can set yourself up to be blessed and at the same time receive favor of all mankind. Take the brakes off, get set and go!

Do Unto Others Before They Do Unto You

No, I didn't get it mixed up. I know exactly what I'm saying, and I am not trying to change what Jesus elaborates on in the Gospel of Luke when He says, "Do unto others as you would have them do unto you." I just wanted to see if you were paying attention, so I decided to add a twist.

Giving and doing special things for others is a great way to get ahead in life. For the next few weeks, go out of your way to send someone something nice for no special reason. Also, while you're at it, give someone a deserving compliment. Drop a gift card in the mail or call someone up and invite him/her over for lunch. Make an effort to make somebody smile. I love trying to beat people to the door so that I can open it for them. Yes, do it to them, not as they would do to you, but before they do it to you, and see how much fun that can be. What a great way to show the love of Christ. Take the brakes off, and go for it!

Tell Your Story for Someone Else's Glory

Have you ever been told, "We're not like you." The first time a child told me that, I was a little puzzled! I thought, "What?!!" She went on to say, "See, we weren't born with money and weren't exposed to people who are different from us, like you were." After questioning the child, I realized that when she made that comment to me, she was not talking about material things. She was talking about my ability to intermingle with people of various races and backgrounds with ease. This was at a time when we were just beginning to integrate the schools, and she said she observed how I got along well with the other races. Her comment made me realize that I had a responsibility to be a model to those that I was in a position to influence because people were looking at me.

It's important to note that she was looking at my behavior, not at anything material. Too often, people look at us and see only what we have. Based on what they see, they make a judgment, and that judgment may be altogether wrong. There's a saying that goes, "If the grass looks greener on the other side, check out the water bill." Regardless of how big your bank account is or how much education you have, what people see may be totally different from what or who you really are. That's why we have to get real. Let people know how you acquired what you have. They need to know that the things that you've acquired didn't appear overnight; you had to work hard for them. Imagine if you were invited to do a presentation, and you were told that you had fifteen minutes to speak about your life.

Let's say the audience saw you drive up in a Benz, walk around adorned in furs and jewelry, and then proceed to the microphone. What would you say about your life? Would you stand there and brag on yourself, telling about how good you are and how much you have? Or would you give someone hope by telling them where you came from and how you made it to the place you are by trusting in God? Think about it…the microphone is in your hand. What are you going to say? Take the brakes off and tell your REAL story for someone else's glory!

Go Out of Your Way for Other People

Always do more than necessary or more than what you have to do, and watch the blessings flow. If you really want to have a good life, stop having the attitude of "it's not my job." You'd be surprised how many opportunities you miss out on by doing the bare minimum.

I was in a restaurant one evening. Although I was seated, it was a long time before the waiter got to me. As a matter of fact, he never got to me; neither did he acknowledge me. It would be wrong for me to assume that he saw me; however, I was sitting between two other tables that he was assisting, and he just walked all around me without speaking or even offering a smile. I was terribly hungry, and as I prayed to God that I would not get upset, a gentleman by the name of Quincy approached me and said, "I see that you've been sitting here for quite some time; what can I do for you?" I asked, "Is this your station?" He answered that it wasn't and pointed to the young man who had walked around me for the last fifteen minutes.

Quincy went on to say, "It doesn't matter to me that this is not my station. I just see you sitting here, and I want to know how I can assist you. I don't mind." He was the answer to my prayer because I was hungry. But he was also the answer to the other waiter's prayer, too because I don't think I was going to be very gracious to him after the way he had snubbed me! Although Quincy did not expect anything in return, I was so grateful that my prayer was answered, I showed my gratitude by giving him a very generous tip, and now we have become the best of friends.

Another example of this attitude of going beyond what is required is in the interactions I had with my mother. My mama and I talked a lot on the phone, and whenever she wanted me to do something she'd say, "Is that going to put you out of your way?" That meant, "I don't want to be a bother." My answer was, "Yes, that's out of my way, but what good is it to me if I don't go out of my way?" My mom raised me to be the woman that I am today, and if I had to go out of my way ten times a day, I'd do it. Yes, you owe people who sacrificed for you or even those who have never done anything for you. If we only did things that were convenient, what good would that be for the Kingdom? So the next time you feel that it's not your job, take the brakes off and go out of your way for somebody. It's worth it, and the rewards are great!

It's Not Who You Know but Who Knows You

I network a lot with my business, and usually when I go to the meetings, I encourage people to say my name aloud. I do that over and over again so that they will know with whom they are speaking when I contact them on the phone. Not only do I want them to remember my name, I also try to remember their names and their product(s) or company so that I can refer others to them. Since the universe works on the law of reciprocity (i.e., what you give out comes back to you multiplied), I try very hard to help others make the connections they need and my efforts always reap benefits.

Let's look at this concept in relationship to our Heavenly Father. We all claim to know God, but do we actually spend enough time with God for Him to really know us? We know that He made us and that He knows our beginning and end. But does He know just how much we really love and trust Him? Some of us only go to God when there's a need or crisis in our life. It is then that some of us beg and plead and make promises that we don't intend to keep. That's why we feel unfulfilled and can't seem to get it together. How can we lead others to Christ if we fail to get to know Him for ourselves? We are put here on this earth to win souls for the Kingdom, and we can't do our networking on Sunday morning in a church building. What have you done lately to win souls for the Kingdom? Are you too busy barely making it yourself? Before you go to the streets, check with your own household. Don't assume that everyone is saved just because you are. Take time to be concerned about your own family first, then move to others. Take the brakes off, and see your life change tremendously. It's never too late!

Show Some Real Love

LOVE is a commandment, not a suggestion and it is the greatest commandment of all. A lot of us are stuck and cannot move on with our lives because we think that we're fooling God about our relationship with our fellowmen. Some people are too self-absorbed, too busy, and too stingy to care for others. Because of that, there's something missing in their lives, but they just can't put their finger on it. There are so many hurting people who need your comfort and encouragement. Yes, comfort and encouragement! Too often, though, we flatter and give empty praise, which is not what people need to hear. People are hurting, and time has passed for being "cutesy, cutesy" and playing games.

Our economy is at an all time low, and we need to be about the business of helping one another, not just making the people feel good for the moment. I could care less about what you have on or what you drive, but what I do care about is what I can do to help you. People who are grounded don't need their egos stroked or a big fuss made over them, but they do need your help if they are hurting.

I visited a church a couple of years ago, and a lady came before the congregation with a testimony about having cancer. She was a beautiful lady, well dressed and very articulate. After the service, I went over and gave her a check to help with her situation. I could have tried to console her by telling her that she still looked good after going through chemotherapy, or that I liked her dress or that I have a relative going through the same thing and I'd be in prayer for her; but how would that have made her situation better? Compliments are nice, but people need substance, and if you can't give money, give your time.

There are many among us who are lonely, have lost jobs or are experiencing broken relationships. And they are not always "other people"; some are in your own family, maybe in your own home. Ask God to open your eyes and your heart to those who need your help. When was the last time you checked on a neighbor or your elderly or ailing parents or siblings? It's not a good idea to wait for family reunions, weddings or funerals to connect and be supportive of one another. We should show love in every way and, if possible, every day.

Think again. When was the last time you helped somebody—I mean, really helped somebody—and didn't want anything in return? That is, you helped, not for show or recognition, but because you saw a need. If you want to receive favor from God, show some love, and help somebody. Take the brakes off, and see how far you'll go! It's awesome!

Gratitude Is Not Silent

Gratitude is one of the most powerful emotions in the world. A grateful heart will open doors beyond belief. When someone shows his/her appreciation towards you, it speaks a whole lot about his character. That person is saying, "I appreciate you," or "thank you."

It seems to be easy for children to openly show gratitude. One of the best feelings that I can receive is for my grandchildren to hug me and say how much they love me when I've done something nice for them, like cooked their favorite meal. The feeling is priceless!

Others, too, like to feel appreciated. How many times have you spent your hard-earned money to do something nice and never received anything in return? Probably, many times—and that's the point. Most businesses take your money for a service, and that's the end of the story, right? Well, one of my clients is an exception. Mitch keeps me busy with my gift basket company by sending gift baskets to his clients. Not only does it keep me busy, but it also keeps the county buzzing with talk about how thoughtful he is and how they can't wait until the next client appreciation party. Mitch really goes all out for his clients, and his clients, likewise, appreciate him. So take the brakes off and remember that gratitude is not silent! Tell or show someone how much you appreciate them.

Don't Keep Score

Even though we all like to be appreciated, remember that whatever you give or do for someone should be done freely from your heart and without any expectation of something in return. You should give generously because God gives us the gift of grace and mercy every day. What if He withheld this gift from you when you didn't acknowledge Him or took Him for granted? When you do for others with the hopes of getting something back or when you try to manipulate someone, you will be disappointed about what you get in return. But John 1:16 says, "From the fullness of grace we have received one blessing after another"—and that's our biggest reward of all.

It's great to have friends that keep in touch no matter what. Vera and Belinda are my former high school classmates, and they are wonderful about calling and sending cards. Belinda sends me a card at least once a month. In fact, I oftentimes go to the mailbox just to check to see if she has sent me one. Vera helps me keep up with everything that's going on with our class. I am really grateful for their attention towards me, and I'm sure there are people for whom you are grateful...and who are gratcful for you.

How often do you keep score after you've called or sent someone something nice? How often have you gotten upset when you didn't get the expected response? Such behaviors are not God's way. We have to remember how many times we have failed to acknowledge what God has done for us, yet He continues to give us the gift of grace and mercy. He doesn't give "tit for tat," and we can't either.

Develop a new attitude towards giving and watch your blessings overflow. Give with love and happiness from your heart because God knows your heart and knows when you are giving begrudgingly. Pray and ask God to open your heart so that you will become a generous giver. God has blessed you to be a blessing to others in some way, so when the blessings begin to flow, take the brakes off, and don't keep score.

Always remember, you cannot navigate through this life without helping someone else. Regardless of how prosperous you may become, your wealth means nothing if you do not have someone to really love you. If you try to create happiness by accumulating wealth, you will never have enough money or feel content. It won't bring you happiness. That's why you should spend your time building relationships where mutual love and respect—and sharing with one another—are evident. Once again, take the brakes off, get set, go and establish loving relationships.

Chapter 5

Pole Position

"So that thou incline thine ear unto wisdom, and apply thine heart to understanding."
~~Proverbs 2:2

Now let's get down to the real nitty-gritty and see how race car terms relate to all of this. Yes, race car drivers use terminology that relates to our everyday life and shows how we can be successful if we take note. So start your engines, and let the race began.

"Pole position" is a term used by race car drivers to see what position they are placed in to compete on the track. Drivers qualify one at a time by taking a lap around the track. The fastest timed car starts first and so forth.

How can we relate this to our own lives and the things that we do on a daily basis? How can we qualify for His loving kindness? God promises us that if we abide in Him and He abides in us, there is nothing that we can ask of Him that He will not deliver. Just as it is with race car drivers and other athletes, promotions on the job or any position that we desire to have, there is always the preliminary round in which to qualify. With the grace of

God and our doing the things that we need to do, we will one day be in a position to live our dream; however, we must realize that our timing is not necessarily God's timing. We just need to stay faithful and hold God to His promise.

Let's look at the word "time" according to Webster. Time is defined as "a particular period or part of duration, whether past, present, or future; a point or portion of duration; as, the time was, or has been; the time is, or will be; a proper time; a season; an opportunity; the duration of one's life; the hours and days which a person has at his disposal."

As stated in Psalms 90:10, God has promised us seventy years here on earth. How are you spending your time? Are you really happy about how your life is going? What can you do to be in a better position to make good on the promise that God has made you in Jeremiah? He said, "For I know the plans I have for you, declares the Lord, plans to prosper you and not to harm you, plans to give you hope and a future." (Jeremiah 29:11 NIV)

Further, Haggai 2:9 (NAS) goes on to tell us, "The latter glory of this house will be greater than the former,' says the Lord of hosts, 'And in this place I will give peace,' declares the Lord of hosts." What God is saying here is that in your last days, He will do great things for you, and He has the resources to give you the best life ever, but He needs you to have a willing heart and some working hands to accept the rewards that He has for you. God can help you, but He will not do it for you. However, what God will do is send people into your life to help guide you and show you the way. God will use every resource in the universe to make good on His promise. That's how much He loves you.

Throughout this book I have shared and will continue to share several ways that you can put yourself in "pole position"—in a position to have the best life possible. However, this chapter is totally dedicated to this end.

Every waking moment, the clock is going tic-tock, tick-tock, tick-tock. Think about this: We have 365 days in the year and 24 hours in each day, but you can't seem to get anything done. As a matter of fact, you seem to be getting further and further behind, and you can never catch up. Whether you're at the office, home or church, you can never seem to get it together. Not only that, but there is still this restless wanderer inside you just begging to get out. You want to do something, but you don't know what it is that you want to do. Or, perhaps, you've got in mind the things that you want to do, but you just can't get that break in life which will allow you to do it. Or maybe you were able to do what you wanted but still got no satisfaction. And last but not least, perchance you've got it all, but you're still not satisfied.

Regardless of your situation, life is in progress, but you feel that it is passing you by. You cannot get back the time that you've lost, but you can make up your mind to either stop or start doing some key things that will put you in a position to live a wonderful, fulfilled life. So let's look at ways that you can put yourself in a fantastic position to receive many blessings.

What You're Waiting for Is Waiting for You

God will never put a thought or an idea in your heart without giving you the ability to make it a reality. Prayer is an important element in getting your heart's desire because as soon as you go to God in prayer, angels are dispatched and ready to go to work on your behalf. They are waiting in every corner of the universe to assist. So when you pray, know that what you're praying for is just around the corner waiting to come your way.

As you work to make your life what you know it can and should be, do not settle for less than you want! Don't let your age be the reason to rush into something. That is, don't think you have to hurry up because you are getting older. Many times, as soon as you rush and do things your way, you discover God had something waiting for you just around the corner, but you missed it. Trust God enough to believe that He can see over the entire universe and bring the perfect situation into your life.

I was visiting a church one day, and as I was sitting enjoying the praise and worship service, a thought ran through my mind. I thought, "God, I love the fellowship so much, but I just wish that somebody from the pulpit really, really knew me, so that whenever my funeral needs to be preached, the eulogist won't have to make up anything." As soon as I had that thought, a young lady got up and opened up the service. She had a dynamic voice and an uplifting message that really inspired me. I didn't have my glasses on, so I called an usher over and asked, "Is that lady named Dee?" He answered by saying, "No, her name is Pastor Luke." I observed Pastor Luke during most of the service, and afterwards, I went down to speak to her. When I got close enough to speak to her, I could not believe my eyes. There she was, all grown up, one of my former basketball players, who is now one of the ministers in the church. She was so excited to see me, and when she introduced me to her colleagues, she told everyone that I was like a second mother to her.

I immediately thought, "God, you just answered my prayer, but I hope you don't think that I am talking about a funeral in the near future!" I share that experience to show that God had Pastor Luke there just waiting for me to ask so that He could show His face. I am sure that I would have seen her eventually, but this was the day that I asked for someone who would know me, and I got what I was asking for. So take the brakes off and know that what you're waiting for is waiting for you!

Don't Overestimate Your Power to Change People

Did you know that only God can change a person's heart? The next time you become frustrated with another adult because you're trying to get him/her to change, realize that you may be wasting your time. Yes, we want to help people, but sometimes doing so can be difficult.

I have known situations where people seriously thought that they could make someone do or be something that the person wanted no part of. Wrong! People are people and do exactly as they please. Often, until they have a life-changing experience, they are going to be pretty much the same. I am not saying that people cannot change, but you can't change them. Only God can. So take the brakes off, and don't overestimate your power to change them!

If You Gotta Dream, Dream Big or Wake Up

Our God is a big God, and He can help us accomplish anything that we set out to do. We need to establish in our hearts what we really want to do, and God will equip us with the resources, finances, and people to assist us. Wake up! Stop saying, "I'll do it later" or "That costs too much." Where is your faith? If you know what you want to do, you've got to act now!

When I think of big dreamers, I think of all of the inventions that have made our lives easier. I think of men and women that have organized groups to help children and others achieve their wildest dreams. Be reminded, though, that God is bigger than any of these! He is rich, and He desires to help us when we make our dreams known to Him. So when you dream, dream big. Take the brakes off or, in other words, wake up!

Don't Let the Arms that Hold You, Hold You Back

Your success in life is 99 percent dependent on the person(s) to whom you attach yourself. People too easily get involved in hopes of having a wonderful relationship and a great future, and when that special person comes along, he/she may forget his/her own dreams. Think about this: since you've met that special someone, are you still pursuing your dream or has that person's dream become yours, too? There is something that God has put in your heart to make you a special individual, and you will not be content until you complete the good work that God started in your life when you were full of energy and vigor. Even if you are not what we would call young anymore, it's not too late to renew your hopes. Share your dream with your loved one. You might be surprised at how he/she will support you. If you don't speak up, though, he/she will never know of your hurt and disappointment. Whether it's going back to school or opening a business, people who love you want you to be successful.

I met Thomas in the ninth grade, and we became a couple. Later, when I went off to college, we communicated back and forth and saw each other during the summer breaks. I remember telling him that I wanted to quit school and get a job. If he had agreed to that, my life would have been much different now. He told me that if I quit school, we wouldn't have a relationship. Again, if people really care about you, they will encourage you to be the best person that you can be. So take the brakes off, and don't let the arms that hold you, hold you back!

Have a Heart of Servitude

I was talking to a friend one day and he said, "Loretta, I just returned from vacation and one thing I can say for sure, when I stepped off of that plane, I knew that I was back in America." My sentiments exactly!!! We in America are always in such a hurry and so busy that we miss some of life's real pleasures. As a result, although

America is known as the land of opportunity, some people would much rather trade places with cultures that are more laid back so they can avoid our hustle and bustle.

Two years ago, I had the opportunity to spend one of the most beautiful vacations of my life with my girlfriend's family in Jamaica. I got the opportunity when I was at a friend's school one day making a delivery. My friend Merlene stuck her head out of her classroom door and said, "Ms. Browning, come go to Jamaica with me." I, of course, said I would. I was pushed for time because she was leaving in two weeks, so I rushed and got my passport, which usually takes six weeks, and got my plane ticket.

I knew that it was going to be a wonderful vacation as my plane flew over the beautiful crystal blue waters and sands of Jamaica. It happened that I arrived one day before Merlene; so her sister and brother-in-law picked me up from the airport. As we left the airport, we went to Pastor Jonathan's house, where I thoroughly enjoyed watching the adults and children laughing and singing together. I didn't hear any loud music, and neither did I see anyone in the room who was not actually involved in what was going on.

There was so much togetherness, and everyone was looking out for the other. Everybody who came through those doors felt as if they belonged—and I felt that way, too. The most memorable part of the entire trip was how Merlene's family went out of their way to make me feel like family. They waited on me and attended to all of my needs; they treated me like royalty, serving me the whole time I was with them. They reflected the true spirit of God, as their love and hospitality encompassed me throughout the entire stay. I even had the opportunity to visit a school that Merlene established in Jamaica. To be among friends and family that share, love and care about each other is a wonderful gift from God.

In order for us to share in the blessings of the Kingdom, we must become servants, like Merlene's family did with me. Regardless of your present situation, take the time out and humble yourself enough to serve others.

Right now I would like to acknowledge my Jamaican family whom I love so much for their warm hospitality and loving spirit: Rosemarie, Pastor Jonathan and Barbara, Joan, Joseph, Roger, Jaunell, Rojaune, Roger (RJ), Kingsley, Grace, Chamarane, Kaje', Candicia, Dr. Jacqueline, Rona, Delores, Noel, Noel Jr., Dr. Antrieve, Dr. Angeline and, of course, Merlene . I encourage you to follow their lead; take the brakes off and have a heart of servitude!

You Can't Do Good and Get Away

Back in 2005 after Hurricane Katrina hit, I went to an administrative building downtown to see if I could get information regarding housing for a few of the children. As I got off of the elevator, there were two young ladies, Kim and Jannicce, who were ready to assist. I told them that I needed to go to the Department of Family and Children Services (DFACS) because I wanted to know if they had enough volunteers to house the victims. They told me that I was not in the right building and gave me directions to DFACS. As I was leaving, they told me that I was in the

Chamber of Commerce building and invited me to a meeting the following day. My being in the wrong building was no coincidence because I had been procrastinating for years about making a decision to join the Chamber of Commerce. I went to the meeting the next day and was more than excited. Everyone had an opportunity to explain their business to the group during the meeting, and I got seventeen leads that day for my gift basket business.

As we were leaving the meeting, I had several business people to approach me for business coaching or the opportunity to assist with managing my business. I had sat next to a lady by the name of Jeffri. When the meeting was over, she quietly said, "Follow me." Jeffri led me to meet Mr. Rod, and eventually I enrolled in his Micro-enterprise Business class where I learned lots of strategies to improve my business.

Since then, we've all become good friends. I do all of the Chamber of Commerce gift baskets and have recently seen several of my baskets on TV. See how God will turn your life around when you set out to help someone else? So take the brakes off and always remember, "You can't do good and get away with it."

Money Talks

I learned this lesson at an early age. Years ago, when I was in middle school, I was awarded a trip to the Junior Olympics in track and field. I was very excited because the trip was out of town, I had never been to another state, and I was even more excited because we had team uniforms with the emblem of the Olympic rings and torch on our crisp, white jackets. I remember the buses loading in the parking lot at Atlanta Stadium and our coaches talking with the news reporters as spectators were waving goodbye. There was so much excitement, but nothing mattered more to me than the fact that I was going on a trip and was going to be away from home for a couple of days.

Then something happened that taught me one of the biggest lessons in the world. Our coach got on the bus and said that the news reporters wanted to talk to one of the team members. He didn't call any names, but I was sure that he was hinting around for me to make my way off the bus. I didn't move because I thought he'd call me up when he wanted me to go out, so I just kept talking to the other kids. Little did I know, he had already chosen the athlete to represent our team. When I looked out of the window, I saw a Caucasian girl laughing and talking to the reporters, shaking hands, and bidding everyone farewell.

As the media were turning off the cameras and we were pulling out for the airport, I asked Coach why he didn't choose me since I was the team captain. In retrospect, I sometimes really hate that I asked that question because it appeared that he had a difficult time giving me the answer. However, he explained to me that we did not have the money to take this trip on our own, so the girl's father had paid for the entire trip for all of us. In other words, her father sponsored the trip. Coach sounded really sad, as if he was trying to apologize to me. However, when he told me that, I turned to the girl and thought, "Thank God for your daddy!"

That was one of the best trips that I've ever had in my entire life, and I tried to make her trip equally as enjoyable because she was the only Caucasian on the team, and some of the kids were not very nice to her. Since then, I have come to realize that money can open many doors, and there are so many times in our lives that we take a lot of things for granted because we feel like we are entitled. We fail to realize that there is someone out there who's paying our way. Likewise, we oftentimes forget that Jesus has already paid our way, but we must always keep that in mind. So the next time you want to be a blessing to others, take the brakes off and remember that sometimes, when we can't pay our own way, money talks!

Let Go and Let God

A couple of years ago, I bought seven African grey geese. They were babies, so I had to put them in a cage for their protection until they got used to their surroundings. After they grew a little, I'd take them out of the cage, let them run around, then cage them again. A couple of weeks after getting them, I had their wings clipped so they wouldn't fly away. Each morning I would go down to the barn and feed them, and I would let them out to run around. A few weeks passed, and I felt as if they were ready to go out on their own, so I let them run around in the yard on their own.

One morning I went down by the pond to feed them, and two were missing; then later on that week, the rest were gone. As I was looking out of my bedroom window later that night, I saw a red fox in my yard and realized that he had killed the geese. That was very painful for me, and I promised God that I would never in my life clip any more wings. I realized that birds are intended to take to the sky; they are meant to fly. That goes for people, too – male, female, child, companion, or business partner. I will never put anyone in a position to force them to stay with me; they need to stay because they want to. Likewise, any man, woman or child who comes into your life must want to stay with you on his/her own; if he/she doesn't, then he/she was not sent to you by God anyway.

Stop trying to make people like you or to keep them tied to you. Stop trying to bribe them with money, nice meals and business deals. You are worthy of the best, so believe that you deserve someone that can give you just as much love as you can give them in return.

Let us look again at the geese story. As soon as I forgave myself and moved on, God sent me two geese that have been with me for the past six months. As a result they have produced five new geese – a total of the seven that I had earlier. And guess what? I didn't have to clip their wings. They can fly away anytime they want to, but they choose to stay. So take the brakes off and let go and let God.

Don't Let Your Feelings Block Your Blessings

When was the last time you had your feelings hurt? Yes, we're all human, and we do have feelings, but don't let your feelings determine your future happiness. When your feelings are hurt, it's only natural that you may pout for a while. However, there are some people that will take the most minor slight to their graves. If that is you, grow up! Yes, grow up and realize that you cannot expect people to always be sensitive to your feelings. Life is too short and people are too busy to have the task of watching what they say and how they behave around you every second of the day.

I've had to tell myself that! One Saturday, I was at a program. Before it began, I went up to shake the pastor's hand. She appeared to have brushed me off and continued to talk to someone else. Yes, my feelings were hurt, and although I didn't know her, I had an attitude towards her. She was the featured speaker, and guess what? Her topic was "Get Your Feelings Out of the Way." I was floored—but happy, too. I am so thankful that I had an opportunity to hear that message because it has changed my life.

My grandchildren used to have the habit of saying, "You hurt my feelings," and I used to pamper them. I don't anymore, though, because I realize that I am fostering a behavior or attitude that will only harm them in the future. You'd be surprised at the good things in life that people have missed out on just because someone hurt their feelings. So take the brakes off, and don't let your feelings block your blessings!

Take Back What the Devil Stole from You?

I put a question mark by this one because sometimes we give too much credit to Satan. Satan does a lot, but we bring a lot on ourselves.

For example, one morning I called a friend, upset about my bank account. I said, "This account is on no digits. What am I to do?" Then I said, "Satan is out to get me!" As we talked and I looked around in the car, I found checks that I had not even deposited—checks that would put some "digits" in that account! Afterwards, I told my friend that every time I set out to do something, the Enemy will come and try to take it away. His response was, "It's not called Satan, Loretta. It's called accounting." So the next time you want to take back what Satan stole from you, check yourself first!

Yes, there are so many, many things that you can do that will definitely put you in a position to be blessed and highly favored. However, we must always remember that we can do nothing alone. All of our help comes from God, and anything outside and apart from God will definitely fail. Go ahead, take the brakes off so that you can be first in pole position.

Chapter 6

Marbles

"Beloved, think it not strange concerning the fiery trial which is to try you, as though some strange thing happened unto you: But rejoice, inasmuch as ye are partakers of Christ's sufferings; that, when his glory shall be revealed, ye may be glad also with exceeding joy."
~~1 Peter 4:12-13

Another word that race car drivers use is "marbles." No, they're not referring to the little glass balls we played with when we were children; this term refers to the debris or obstacles on the track which make it dangerous to compete. Marbles are usually small chunks of tires and anything else that comes off of the race car as it speeds around the track.

In everyday life, sometimes we procrastinate or postpone a project because of the obstacles that we face. I can assure you that when you set out to do something worthwhile, it won't be as easy as you think; you will encounter obstacles. The finished product may look like making it was easy, but every successful outcome has a story behind it; so, here's mine.

When I began this project, a publishing company gave me books so that I could review some of their work. They allowed me to take the books home, and I promised that I would take good care of them and return them in a couple of days. During that time, my daughter Thomi called and asked if I could keep the children while she and her husband Darrell went on a date, and I agreed to do so.

Later during the week as I left my house to return the books, I discovered the books were not in the back seat of my car where I thought I had left them. I ran back inside to look on my dresser, but still there were no books. I immediately picked up the phone and called Thomi, asking her if I had left the books on the counter at her house since I'd taken them there when I babysat the kids. Darrell said that the books weren't there, but I called back a second time and asked if he would please check again. The answer was still the same. By now, I began to get really nervous, because these books were put into my care with the promise of a safe return.

Suddenly I thought, "The trash! It's trash day!" I had not put the trash on the street in a couple of weeks, but, of all days, I decided to put it out that day! I thought, "I accidentally put the books in the trash, and now they are gone forever." In a panic, I called the sanitation department to see what area of the dump they would have taken my trash. I pictured myself standing on mounds and mounds of stinky trash all by myself searching for the books because I knew that nobody loved me enough to go there and pull through trash with me. (You can see here that Satan can get you running all over the place looking silly. He can actually have you wallowing in trash if you're not careful.) The sanitation department, however, was of little help. When I hung up from the sanitation department, I called my friend for a short second to tell of my situation. Completely frustrated, I could feel tears begin to well up in my eyes. When I hung up, I screamed at the top of my voice, "WHEN THE RUBBER MEETS THE ROAD, IT'S ONLY ME AND GOD!" And guess what happened? As soon as I surrendered and called out for help from the Almighty, I flopped down on the bed, leaned back, and put my hand on the books that were tucked away under my pillow. Unbelievable—but true! When things go bad, as they often will, remember that God can help when no one else can. Yes, when the rubber meets the road, it's only you and God.

I don't know if anyone would have stood on those mounds of trash with me that day, and I'm not even sure I would do the same for anyone else if the situation had been reversed. However, one thing I do know for sure is that God will be there when no one else will. I also know that His love and overflowing power can help you overcome every single obstacle in your life.

The Bible says that Jesus has come so that we might have life and have it more abundantly. Another scripture goes on to say that Satan comes to steal, kill and destroy. Which scripture do you choose to believe? You seriously need to believe both. We just can't pick part of the Bible and put our faith in whichever scripture we choose to believe. We have to believe it all.

One of the scriptures which I believe captures the essence of what I am saying throughout this book is

Ephesians 6:10-12, which says: "Finally, be strong in the Lord and in His mighty power. Put on the full armor of God so that you can take your stand against the devil's schemes. For our struggle is not against flesh and blood, but against the rulers, against the authorities, against the powers of this dark world and against the spiritual forces of evil in the heavenly realms." This scripture tells us that there will always be a struggle in our lives between good and evil, and we need to know the truth so that we can be ready to defend ourselves. If we do not believe that the devil is real and do not have a divine connection with God, we will not be able to overcome obstacles that are placed before us.

The scriptures tell us that whenever there is a crisis in our lives, we need to be equipped to fight the battle. I really think that a lot of people who go to church confuse it with being saved. They feel that since they tithe, work on the usher board, sing in the choir or treat everyone nicely, they're going to see heaven's door. However, many of them won't because as soon as trouble comes along, they find that they do not have the equipment to fight Satan, and they fall by the wayside. Also, some Christians think that because they are saved, they are supposed to struggle while here on earth. Yes, there will be difficult times, but "troubles don't last always." We will overcome because we are witnesses for Christ, and as overcomers, we should have a testimony.

Additionally, some Christians live a life of low self-esteem because they haven't mustered the power to defeat the enemy. Scripture speaks to these Christians, saying that power comes when the Holy Spirit comes into their life. It says in Acts 1:8: "But ye shall receive power, after that the Holy Ghost is come upon you: and ye shall be witnesses unto me both in Jerusalem, and in all Judea, and in Samaria, and unto the uttermost part of the earth." Just imagine how awesome and how powerful our lives would be if we decided to surrender our lives to the Holy Spirit.

Surrendering to the Holy Spirit, however, means that we know Him. Acts 19:14-15 tells about a team of Jews who were going around town experimenting with casting out demons by mimicking Paul. As they approached a demon-possessed man and tried to cast the demon out, the demon inside of the man responded, "Jesus I know, Paul I know, but who are you?" The demon-possessed man leaped on two of them, and beat them so terribly that they ran out of the house injured and naked.

Just as the demon-possessed man recognized a fake, so does Jesus. The same kind of thing can occur in our lives when we try to call on His name but have not established a relationship with Him. He will not know us and will leave us feeling weak and defeated. That is why we fail to overcome obstacles in our lives. To change this, get to know God, and ask Him to allow the Holy Spirit to rest upon you because that is where your strength comes from.
I was talking to a friend one evening, and she shared with me all of the dreams that she had when she was younger. She's about five years my junior.

As we talked, her entire conversation went something like this: "I was going to do this, but…, I could have done that, but… I should have done, but…." When I asked her why she had changed her mind about working toward her goals, she responded that she was getting "on up in age." It's sad but so true that her day may never come. So many times, people, like my friend, will set out to accomplish a dream, but when their lives take different directions, they either put their dreams on hold or give up altogether. Remember, there's always something to keep us from doing what we feel we need to—maybe marriage, children, career, finances, or whatever.

Some of you may be in a situation where you started out with one dream in mind, but you've changed your mind. That's okay for now; however, keep dreaming and refuse to give up. Whatever you do, keep the faith, and believe that when God put that desire in you to open that business, write that book or to further your career or education, He also equipped you with the people and the resources to fulfill your dream, and you'll get it right one day.

I would like to emphasize how God will send people into your life to help you carry out His assignment. This project has not been easy for me. My biggest obstacle has been with the computer. Even though I believe that this is a God-given assignment, I was thinking about giving up, and I was only one chapter short of completing this project. When I got up one morning, I could not find my information on the computer, and I panicked. I called a friend who lived over 300 miles away, and he walked me through the process of regaining my information.

When you are on a mission to do what is good in the sight of God, He will commission people from every corner of the world to help with His plan for your life. But you have to remember this: "They that wait upon the LORD shall renew their strength; they shall mount up with wings as eagles; they shall run, and not be weary; and they shall walk, and not faint." (Isaiah 40:31)

We sometimes abort our own dreams and put plans that God has for our lives on hold because we become frustrated with our conditions and afraid that things are not going to work out for us. But strive to be like the eagle. An eagle never has the same air under his wing; there's something different everyday. That's the way we can expect our lives to be. God has given us the authority over any difficulty that we may encounter.

If we could glance into the spirit realm, we would be astonished. God has angels sitting ready to take our lives to the next level. What are you waiting for? We all face difficulties and challenges in life, and we may be tempted sometimes to give up when we experience difficulty. But remember, as a believer, you have the power to change the course of history. Have you heard media mogul Tyler Perry's story about the setbacks that he endured in his life and how he became homeless? Even in that condition, Mr. Perry wasn't walking around in a daze; he continued to try and try until doors finally opened for him. Now, look at what he has accomplished in the film industry.

Not only does Satan attempt to attack individuals, but he aims to destroy their families as well. When Satan is attacking one person and his/her dreams, his mission is to destroy that person's entire household, especially the head of the household which should be the male. In 2009 on his website, Tyler Perry recounted how, until he was nineteen years old, he suffered routine beatings and profanity at the hands of his father. See how Satan used the father to attempt to destroy Mr. Perry's dream? But he didn't; Mr. Perry prevailed.

Yes, Satan wants the head; he wants to strike the head and, thus, kill the body. Satan could care less whether or not you get that promotion or buy a new house. His main goal is to keep you busy and in debt so that you won't have time to enjoy life. He wants to frustrate you to the point that your household becomes dysfunctional and you continue to pass that cycle from generation to generation. I urge you to have a plan for Satan. When obstacles come your way, put your plan in place by arming yourself with prayer. Pray as a family, getting everyone involved in prayer time. Pretty soon, Satan will flee and go knocking at someone else's door.

Regardless of the circumstances, you need to believe that God will do great things in your life. Don't believe me? Look at the obstacles these people had to overcome.
- Ray Charles, legendary music artist, was told to weave chairs because he couldn't sing.
- Mary Kay Ash, founder of Mary Kay, was told by her attorney to count her losses, recoup her cash, and get out of the business.
- Nelson Mandela, former President of South Africa, spent 27 years in prison but was later elected President, won the Nobel Peace Prize, and is now spending the remainder of his life dedicated to ending apartheid in South Africa.

- Michael Jordan, famed basketball player, was cut from his high school basketball team, later becoming the number one basketball player in the world.
- Clark Gable, famous actor, was told by Hollywood critics that he would never have the opportunity to play "the leading man," but history tells us that he became known as Rhett Butler in Gone with the Wind.
- Dr. Seuss' books were rejected 23 times before they were accepted by publishers; the 24th said yes.
- Dr. Wayne Dyer's childhood was spent in foster homes, but now he is a world-wide speaker with self-help books that have helped millions of people.
- Ray Kroc sold paper cups to support his family, and later he began selling milk shake machines. Then at age 52, as he was trying to sell a milk shake machine to the McDonald brothers, he visualized the great opportunities for franchising, bought the rights to start his franchise, and built a multi-billion dollar business in just 22 years.

And the epitome of achieving despite obstacles is our nation's 44th President, Barack Obama. President Obama and our First Lady, Michelle Obama, did not win the election by focusing on past hurts, insults and humiliation. They worked for what they have gotten! They have inspired many of us to keep moving gracefully toward improving and believing.

Like all of the persons mentioned, you can accomplish great things in your life when you move beyond the "marbles" and other distractions that threaten to knock you off track and impede your progress.

Let's now look at a few ways that can make our travel through life less complicated.

Watch What You Say

I was at the movies years ago watching the movie The Titanic. In the movie, as people were boarding the ship, the owner of the Titanic casually said, "Not even God can sink this ship." Clearly, he underestimated the power of God. Like the owner of the Titanic, there are things we say without realizing how those idle words can be harmful to our success. Look at the statements below:

- You make me sick.
- You're going to be the death of me yet.
- I'm broke.
- You get on my nerves.
- You ain't no good.
- You're bad.
- Drop dead.

Years back, a 21-year-old man killed his father. When this incident hit the media, reporters interviewed people in the man's neighborhood. They said that when this child was a little boy, the father would always tell him, "Son, you're going to be the death of me, yet." A lot of neighbors said that every time they spoke with the father, he'd say the same thing over and over again—i.e., that his son would be the death of him. Well, surely enough that's exactly what happened. See, we need to be very careful with our words. Stop saying things that can put a halt to your future.

One morning as I was walking out to feed my animals, my dog Rocky, a little Yorkshire terrier, was rushing in front of me to run to the mailbox. I yelled out, "Rocky, somebody's going to steal your little tail." As soon as I made that statement, someone stopped at my mailbox and instantly scooped him up! So the next time you get ready to speak, take the brakes off, and watch what you say!

Play Hide and Seek

Unhappy and unlucky people will always be a part of our society, but you must avoid them before you become one of them. You have wasted enough time listening to stories about how badly everyone is treating them. Unhappiness is contagious. The more you listen to unhappy people, the more you will be like them. You might have attempted to tell these people over and over again that things will work out in their lives, but with them, it's always something. And when it's not something, they'll make up something.

We live in a spirit world, and spirits need a human body to possess. Don't let your body become the dwelling place of negative spirits. Avoid them at all cost, and seek out wholesome relationships with people who have positive things going on in their lives. You'd be surprised at how much better you'll begin to feel about yourself when you separate yourself from them. Take the brakes off, and seek wholesome relationships!

Don't Join the "Barely Making It" Club

Life is too short and time is passing too fast to become a member of the "Barely Making It" Club. What is this club? The "Barely Making It" Club is where everyone complains about everything, and everyone is satisfied with nothing. When you ask someone in the Club, "How are you doing today?" they reply, "Oh, I'm barely making it." The members try very hard to recruit members because misery loves company.

Abraham Lincoln said, "Most folks are about as happy as they make up their minds to be." Get in the habit of speaking positively about situations, yourself and other people. Speak healing, wellness and prosperity. Whatever you do, take the brakes off and don't join the "Barely Making It" Club.

Don't Meet Them at the Water Fountain

We spend a lot of time at work, and every once in a while, we've got to take a break. There are some areas in the building where people go to vent and gossip, and we've coined that place "the water fountain." Warning: Don't go there! Why? Because what you say there will spread all over the building before you can get back to your desk!

Yes, talk gets around, and the sad part of it is that the leader of those at the water fountain is the one who's spreading the rumors and associating your name with them. Have you ever wasted energy wondering why someone engaged you in conversation, then took an innocent comment that you made and turned it into an outright lie! It was almost like the other person tricked you into saying something they could build upon and make sensational. Some things can be avoided, and this is one. You're the only one who can control this situation. Stop wasting time around the water fountain. Keep people out of your business, and stay out of theirs.

It's estimated that Corporate America loses billions of dollars each year on people who are unproductive on the job. Don't be one of them. Don't hang out with the slackers at lunch or even sit at the same table with them. Don't let them pull you into conversations about your supervisors—or, for that matter, about anyone. Next time you have a break, take the brakes off, and don't meet them at the water fountain!

Don't Be a Talebearer

Likewise, don't be a talebearer. I shudder to think of what turn the history of our world would have taken if Phillip had been a talebearer. Remember in the Bible when Jesus went into Galilee, found Phillip and told Phillip to come with him? Phillip was so excited that he went to find Nathanael. With much excitement, he told Nathanael that he had found the Messiah! Nathanael remarked, "Can anything good come out of Nazareth?" That remark alone could have been enough for a talebearer (troublemaker) to run with and start some gossip.

Have you ever listened to negative things that someone has said about others? Then, have you ever called someone to tell him/her what someone else had said? I have known of situations where people have stopped speaking to their friends or walked around for years with a grudge because they thought someone said something negative about them. And the reality is that what was said wasn't even true, or the truth had been distorted. Usually, the talebearer is the one who pretends to keep the peace among the group by going from one individual to the other carrying or bringing messages.

When I was a school administrator, I told some of my staff that if they had a complaint or an issue with someone that they would have to bring that person along to my office in order for me to entertain the situation. These were teachers who wanted to tell me what was going on but, at the same time, wanted to remain anonymous. That kind of thing causes a lot of confusion and wastes a lot of time. If people know that you will search for the truth, they will not bring gossip to you. Carrying stories is a waste of time and energy. So take the brakes off; be like Phillip and don't be a talebearer.

<u>Let 'Em Talk</u>

When I was growing up, my mama would say, "Don't give people anything to talk about." I understood what she meant by that. In other words, do the best that you can so people won't have anything bad to say about you. Again, I thought that was pretty good advice, but we all know that it doesn't matter how good or bad you are, people will talk regardless, even if they have to make something up.

A couple of years ago, while I was watching the Fantasia Barrino story, there was a part in the movie where the *American Idol* staff called Fantasia into the office and shared with her some of the things that the spectators were saying about her. They suggested that the viewers did not agree that she should be a contestant on the show because she had a child out of wedlock. They finally said, "Fantasia, people are talking." Fantasia pondered what they said for a few minutes, then looked them straight in the eyes and said, "Let 'em talk."

Can you imagine how things would have been for Fantasia if she had listened to people and given up her dream? There's another saying that goes, "Let's give 'em something to talk about," and that's what she did. I was at the grocery store last year and saw Fantasia coming out of the store. I hollered at her, and she ran over and hugged my neck. She was looking good. I am so happy she followed her heart to not let people dictate her future. Can you imagine how many people are living an unfulfilled life by being too careful in an effort to prevent other people from talking about them?

The other day the news reported that President Obama and our First Lady Michelle Obama went on a date. The media was all in an uproar about tax dollars being wasted on their night out. I am a taxpayer, and if my taxes have to go up because of this one incident, so be it. The First Lady looked gorgeous! This couple has changed the face of history and they deserve to have what is owed to the both of them for being our leaders. They may have been the subject of talk...but who cares?

Further, one day a girl walked into my home as I was looking at Oprah. She said, "I don't like her." "Why?" I asked. Her response was, "She doesn't do anything to help black people." I wasn't comfortable with that comment, so my response to her was that Oprah doesn't owe us anything. She can do whatever she pleases with her own money. However, if the girl had done her research, she'd know that Oprah is one of the most generous women in the world, giving liberally to all kinds of people—including black people.

Let people talk...but ignore what they say. Just be the person that God has intended for you to be, and be supportive and loving of each other's accomplishments. Go ahead; take the brakes off and let 'em talk! And yeah, give 'em something to talk about!

Yes, there are so many things that we can do to navigate our course with fewer obstacles. However, most of our problems come as a result of our own insecurities and the way that we handle situations. If we strive towards wisdom and truth and avoid many of the foolish negative forces that we allow to take up most of our time, we will be surprised at how much we can accomplish. So take the brakes off and avoid the marbles.

Chapter 7

Draft

"Dear brothers, what's the use of saying that you have faith and are Christians if you aren't proving it by helping others? Will that kind of faith save anyone?"
~~James 2:14

In addition to the term "marbles" that we discussed in the previous chapter, another term that race car drivers use is "draft." Drafting is simply following; however, drafting is following from a scientific angle. When race car drivers follow cars as close as possible, it can reduce wind resistance, conserve fuel and build up speed. In life, we can liken drafting to someone going before you in order to help you accomplish your dreams with as few problems as possible.

Take a good look at your life. You're doing fine, huh? You have a nice family, a good job, a nice business, money in the bank, and plenty of friends. I'm sure you know that whatever you've accomplished in life, even if you are not satisfied with your level of accomplishment, was achieved because someone helped you get there.

Life is always in progress...so take the breaks off

I mentioned Fantasia Barrino earlier. Fantasia is an example of how a single individual, sometimes a person you don't even know, can change your life for the better. In Fantasia's story, the American Idol winner recounted how she was about to turn back and go home rather than compete on American Idol because she was too late to go inside, but a security officer allowed her to enter after the doors were shut. What a talent the world would've missed if it weren't for that one kind act on the guard's part.

Tyler Perry is another example. I remember hearing on numerous occasions that Tyler said that a lady he didn't know helped him with shelter while he was down and out and that she was one of the reasons for his success. Praise God for the kindness of others!

As we reflect on our lives, we should show gratitude for people who helped us get to where we are today. Begin by thinking about your ancestors and others from times past who paved the way for you to be where you are. Think about your grandparents who babysat when your mom and dad had to work. Don't forget your parents who worked hard to give you opportunities they never had. There were so many people who made sacrifices so that you could be better off than they were. The next time you're at a family reunion, look around and thank God for your family.

Then think about the corner grocer who gave you your first job. Think about that spouse who sacrificed his/her own career for yours and for the family. Think of the person who supported your vision for that business venture. Where are these people now? Then think about how much you have given back? You may not necessarily have the opportunity to give back to them directly, but it is your responsibility to "pay it forward" and give someone else a helping hand.

Just as a team is important in auto racing, in order for you to move on with your life, it is very important to be a part of the right team. Notice that I said the right team. Toxic relationships will keep you in bondage, making you second guess your real purpose in life and stagnate your dreams to the point that you will eventually lose hope. You don't need anyone on your team who will hinder your progress.

Usually, your family is a big part of your team. When we were coming up as children, some of us had big dreams and felt that we could take on the world. We felt that our parents didn't understand us because they taught us to get a good job with benefits, and that was all there was to it. Some of you did as they said, and some didn't. Some of you who haven't achieved all you want are still angry that your parents did not buy into your big vision. If that is what happened to you, let it go. They only did what they thought was best for you at the time. Remember, you still have a shot at accomplishing your heart's desire, so don't give up on your dream. You're still here, and it's never too late to rekindle that dream.

In your efforts to move ahead, I'm sure you have encountered people who really want to hold you back. They don't want to see you happy or successful. Regardless of what you do, they belittle your efforts and will do anything to steal your joy. Some of these people can be family members—people who should be on your team but aren't. But you can't allow them to shape your future. Don't let them win. Thank God for putting them in your life because it was a part of His plan to bring out the best in you. Move on, and let your haters be your motivators.

Don't confuse the haters with people who just want to see you do your best. They may criticize, but their reason for doing so is different from that of the haters. People who care about you will tell you the truth. Whether it's your hairstyle, clothes, behavior or whatever else you may need advice on, people who have your best interest at heart will be up front and honest. If you ask a "real" friend, don't be hurt if you get a "real" answer. It's the "yes" people who could care less, so don't expect much fuss from them. Even when President Obama picked his Cabinet, he based his choices on people who were not afraid to disagree with him. Don't be afraid to follow his lead. Make sure your team has on it people who are not afraid to be frank so that you can become the best you can be.

Still other people on your team will obviously show their support of you. Their role in "drafting" will help you achieve at the highest level. I'll share a personal example of drafting as it relates to my career as an educator. Several years ago, I ran across a former associate superintendent who had tried to encourage me to go into administration when I first started with the school system. When I later told him that I was finally ready, he was very kind in making a commitment to help me as much as possible and asked me to come see him. When I went to see him, he reminded me of the days when he would come into my classroom to observe, and he mentioned that he admired the way I gave of myself to the teaching profession. He reminded me of how he had tried to encourage me years earlier to go into administration but that I had told him that I enjoyed what I was doing at the time. He told me stories of how hard early educators had fought to get quality administrative positions in the county, and he named quite a few people he personally had helped along the way. He said that he wanted me to get an appointment with the central office and to let them know that he had sent me to see them.

I did what he said. The people whom he sent me to see knew absolutely nothing about me, but what they did know was that this man had helped them, and for that reason, they felt that it was their duty to help me. In fact, one lady he sent me to see got a little choked up when she remembered that this man was why she was where she was. When she sent me to see someone else in the personnel office, that person said the same thing about the man who had started the ball rolling for me. She told me, "I am going to help you because this man helped me; that's the least that I can do." She also went on to say, "You'll be an assistant principal now, but we'll give you three years then make you a principal." This experience of mine is a good example of how people can open doors and clear a path for you, but you have to make sure that you are prepared when that time comes.

The Bible says that your latter days will be better than your first, and God really proved Himself on this one when I was hired as an administrator because I had the opportunity to work with some of the best people in the world. We had the best staff and best leadership team you could find anywhere because we all helped one another by working together as a team. The author John Maxwell seemed to describe us in his book entitled Teamwork Makes the Dream Work. Our team consisted of our head counselor; the administrators, including our dynamic principal; and a few incredibly strong teachers. We would start our Monday mornings before school with prayer behind closed doors in the principal's office. Sometimes when we'd finished and I walked into the front office with my face full of tears, parents and teachers thought that I was having a distressed moment; little did they know that the very opposite was true.

Other great team members included our plant engineer, our security desk attendant, and our security officer. Together, we worked and kept things running smoothly. Andrew Carnegie said it best when he said, "It marks a big step in your development when you come to realize that other people can help you do a better job than you could do alone." We knew that and had some wonderful times back then. I thank God that He loved me enough to bring them into my life. But the whole story started with one man who had enough confidence and faith in me from the beginning. Even when I was comfortable with the way that my life was going, he kept encouraging me to reach my full potential, and I am grateful to him.

You have to be grateful for those who help you, and one way to show your thanks is to reach back and pull someone up the ladder with you. God will always put people in your path so that you can be a blessing to them. That's why you must always be on the lookout for someone you can help in order to make his/her life easier. That's what God is all about. We are put here on this earth to help one another. I try to do that.

An example of that is seen when I was appointed to be in charge of the Black History program. On the day of the program, I panicked because I needed one more participant and did not know whom I could ask. Finally, I decided to ask Teresa, a member of our auxiliary staff. However, she said that she did not have the time in her schedule because she had an appointment later on that evening and had to finish her portion of work at the school. I begged and promised that I would help her finish her work if she took part, and finally she agreed to do so. I was so grateful.

Later, I remembered that Teresa had informed me some time back that she had her credentials to be a secretary. At the time she told me that, I really didn't pay that much attention because there were not any openings available. However, after spending time with her that evening, I realized what a hard worker she was. Not only was she a hard worker, but her attitude toward the administration and the children was one to be admired. Later that same week, I had a talk with her and asked if she wanted me to recommend her to become my secretary since an opening had just become available. Not only did she accept the position, but she continues to be outstanding in the position.

Oftentimes when I read Jeremiah 29:11, I wonder how many believers will stake claim to that awesome promise. God says in that scripture, "...I know the plans I have for you...plans to prosper you and not to harm you, plans to give you hope and a future." There have been circumstances in my life when God has sent people from every corner of the world to make my path clear. His plans for me gave me "hope and a future." A lot of times, we look at things from a natural perspective. We look at our circumstances, our present situation, and we get frustrated. But we know that God is the Truth, and He will not lie.

He promised us in His Word that His plans are good for us, and I believe those plans include sending people to help us. And when people come into your life to support your dream, let them. Learn how to receive their help. Your dreams might require more money, more time and more resources than you could ever imagine—but God has someone out there who is willing to make an investment in you—and you, in turn, can make an investment in someone else. Always remember, anytime you can help somebody, do it, because regardless of where you are in life, somebody has helped you.

In the sections below, we will discuss how to develop and maintain good wholesome relationships with people that have been a blessing in your life.

Dig Your Well Before You're Thirsty

Digging your well before you are thirsty simply means that you should make preparations before there's a need. Of all of the people in the world, you should have at least one person on whom you can depend, based on the fact that, from previous experience, they know they can depend on you. Relationships should not be one-sided. People need each other, but the problem comes into play when one person feels as if he/she is being taken advantage of.

That's the way God sometimes feels about us. At times, we are so busy and only go to Him when there's an emergency. We tire ourselves out by trying to work out situations until we are desperate; then we turn to God. Yet, He is always there for us. Even though we've taken advantage of him, He forgives us; He loves us, listens to us, and is there for us when no one else is left to talk to. If we really want that type of relationship with God, we should take the brakes off and dig our well before we're thirsty!

Keep in Touch with People Who Helped You

It's important that you remember people who helped you reach your goals in life. That's something that I taught both of my girls. Gratitude is so important, and the rewards are tremendous. Never forget those who helped you. There are several people I'll never forget...people with whom I'll always stay in touch. Among them are the following.

Ethel and E.C. are my daughters' godparents. During the early years, they spent much time helping with everything that was needed. Our biggest celebration of the year was on Christmas Eve when they'd come over and open gifts with the children. Although we don't get together as much as we used to anymore, we still keep in touch.

Also, years back, I had two girls to come live with me. They still keep in touch, and it blesses me when they invite me out or come to visit.

My girlfriend Gayle is awesome. I met her on the campus of Morris Brown College, and she became one of my dear friends. She's bright, honest, and caring. I can never repay her for the many nice things that she did for me when we were young adults. Although we don't talk as much as we used to, we still keep in touch with each other from time to time.

I met Loaird at Tennessee State years ago. He married my roommate Pat, and we were like a team. He was always looking out for me like he would a sister, and we became close friends. It's good to have friends, but it's even better to let them know how much you appreciate them. I make sure I let him know that every once in awhile.

Mack is another person with whom I try to maintain contact. Usually, when I go through the airport, I stop in his restaurant and leave a note for him. One time, as a joke, I left him a couple of bucks to buy himself a chicken biscuit from his own restaurant. I try to call occasionally, and when he's too busy to return my call, I'll drop him a card in the mail.

When people help you, your responsibility is to remember and give back. Sometimes you may wonder how you can give back if the person appears to already have it all. But don't worry about that. Just do your part, and God will do the rest.

Yes, real gratitude remembers. So take the brakes off, and keep in touch with people who've helped you!

Stop Hating

When I was a child, I had a friend, Deborah, who lived directly across the street from me. Deborah was very nice and was quiet, and we had a lot of fun playing together. She lived with her grandparents, and it appeared that she was much better off than the rest of the children in the neighborhood.

There was another girl a little older who would come over to play with the both of us from time to time, and it appeared that she and Deborah were very close. However, one day, I found that this other girl was not at all the type person she should be.

That day when we were visiting, Deborah took us into the bedroom to show us her Blue Bird uniform. It was a dark blue skirt, hat and vest. I was really happy for her because, although I was in the same group, I did not have a store-bought uniform, and I thought that hers was really neat. After admiring the uniform, we went to the front porch. Shortly afterward, Deborah's friend went inside. A short time later, I asked Deborah if I could use the restroom, and she allowed me to do so. As I passed through the bedroom, I saw the other girl pouring baby powder on Deborah's dark blue skirt, then attempt to destroy the hat. Not only was I shocked, I was scared! Since it was sort of dark in the house, everything appeared to be turning a little weird. I ran outside and told Deborah what the girl had done, and she said that the girl had done things like that before. I did not understand why because both Deborah and her grandmother were nice and always tried to help people. I was really confused. Apparently, that "friend" was filled with hatred and/or jealousy toward Deborah, but Deborah allowed her to visit just like I did. Deborah knew what the girl was like yet had made a decision to keep her as a friend.

Some of you might be like Deborah's friend, hateful and filled with jealousy. Realize, though, that jealousy is like poison and when you ingest, it will destroy your life in ways never imagined. Right now, make a decision to be more like Deborah, whose heart was large enough to accept a friend who meant her no good. Stop causing heartache and pain, especially to those who have no idea that you're out to get them; stop the fake smiling face; stop the fake hugs. The Bible describes that kind of behavior as heaping coals of fire on your own life. So take the brakes off, and stop hating!

Get Involved and Know Your Community

Here I want to share with you the power that unity brings. When President Obama was campaigning for President, I called the headquarters and asked how I could assist. They gave me the assignment of knocking on doors, but I found it to be too hot to walk the streets. Then, I was given the assignment of making phone calls. That wasn't going fast enough because every time I spoke to an elderly person, I would stay on the phone too long with them praising God and saying, "We never thought we'd see this day." So that didn't work either, but I still wanted to help.

I went to the front desk and told the administrator that I was going to make up my own campaign job, and I would call to let her know my progress. I decided to have a block party on my front lawn and invited everyone that I could think of. I also put a huge sign out front that read, "If you are reading this, you are invited." I went around to all of the local stores and asked for donations, and Mudea's Soul Food and Blimpie gave generous donations. The party was a huge success! We registered voters, and the neighbors got to meet each other—and we haven't stopped socializing with each other. I started a group called Grassroots Neighborhood Connect, and we meet twice a year to mix and mingle. Afterwards, each individual subdivision goes back to its own group and has its own meeting. Since then, we have gotten to know one another, everyone is more sociable, and we're all working towards a better community.

We try to work closely as a community, and we've included the local high school. We have gotten to know the faculty and staff, and the principal is very supportive of what we are doing.

Additionally, out of Grassroot Neighborhood Connect, another group was formed called Sista, Sista. The members of that group and I meet every first Sunday for dinner, and we bring our special dishes, chat, play games, watch movies and have vowed to be there for each other forever!

Not only have we gotten to know as many people in your community as possible, but we have tried to re-create the days when people were just friendly to one another. I know my bankers personally; I buy the sanitation workers lunch from time-to-time and always give them and the mailman a Christmas gift. I know the UPS man, and when I go to the Y.M.C.A. in the mornings, I am greeted with a friendly smile by the lady who works behind the counter. I am putting myself out to know my neighbors, even when they don't actually live in my community.

Finally, I keep in touch with friends who live in my old neighborhood, sometimes inviting them to join in my new neighborhood gatherings. You can do all of this, too! Just take the brakes off, and get involved with your community!

Be the Boss

Being in charge gives you a great opportunity to bless someone else's life. Look at the President of the United States. Even in his high position, he allows the children of the White House staff to use the play set that was built for his two girls. That's the type of consideration that makes others want to be a part of your team.

Being the boss does not mean bossing people. Look at your leadership style and see if you are the type of supervisor for whom you'd like to work. Are you always complaining? Are you inconsiderate of others and their family members? Is your staff overworked and underpaid? Or are you sensitive and considerate, understanding those under you and wanting to make the workplace as pleasant as possible? God is very concerned about how you treat people who are under your care, and He will reward your success accordingly.

Remember, having power is nowhere near as important as what you choose to do with it. So take the brakes off, and be the boss—but a good boss!

People Want to Feel Needed

From time to time, you may have a need for someone's assistance, so don't be afraid to ask. There are a lot of people out there just waiting to help. A lot of people feel that they are useless, maybe because they are elderly or not well; they can become depressed and withdrawn, but you might be just the one to give them a reason for being.

I recently read an article which shows an example of this. It said that an elderly lady had to move in with her daughter because of health reasons. Although she was instructed to stay off her feet and get plenty of bed rest, she decided to prepare meals for the family because she wanted something to do. Understandably, the daughter was disturbed because the mother was not following doctor's orders. However, the mother continued preparing dinner for the family on a daily basis. The mother was so happy that the grandchildren and the daughter appeared to need her services that she was on her feet and off the medication within a couple of months. The mother is back at home now but insists that the family still needs her services. So she's there once a week preparing meals for the whole family. So, take the brakes off, and realize that people want to feel needed!

This goes for children, too. Sometimes they feel that they are too small to help. They want to contribute to the household, but they don't know what to do. Think of some things that you can allow your kids to do to make them feel as if they are very much needed in order to keep the family going. An example of my doing that occurred one day when I was at a high school doing some volunteer work. I had my grandson William with me. Initially, William was excited to be in the room as we were preparing breakfast for the teachers, then he became irritable and wanted to go home. In trying to coerce him to stay, I started giving him some tasks to do. The more responsibility that I gave him, the happier he appeared, and as time went on, William started making up his own projects and doing things on his own. At one point the little man was unstoppable.

Remember, everyone needs something to do! So, take the brakes off, and help people feel that they are needed!

Teach Your Children These Two Things

I have two daughters, and early in their lives, I gave them two pieces of advice, and I really feel that they listened to me. First, I told them to stick together at all costs. If you allow your kids to physically fight in front of you or allow them to mistreat each other, you are allowing them to develop negative lifelong habits. Sibling relationships are very important and should be cultivated and nurtured throughout the years.

The other advice that I gave my daughters was to observe how I treated my mom and treat me accordingly. When my mom was living, I called her at least ten times a day and was always excited to do whatever I could for her. She once told me that I was going to live a long time like my uncle Thomas because I was always there for her. Now, my girls don't call me ten times a day, but they do call every day, and the grandkids do the same, and I appreciate that. They give me gifts, they're concerned when I have problems, and they always encourage me. I wasn't the best mother that I could have been because there's always room for improvement, but we love each other, and we have a wholesome relationship. It just makes me feel so good to see them getting together, going out and having fun like sisters and friends. So take the brakes off, and teach your children those things that will bring a smile to your face.

Train Up Your Child

There is a story in Aesop's Fables entitled *"A Young Thief and His Mother"*. As the story goes, a young thief was caught stealing and was about to be executed. Before execution, though, he asked the authorities if he could speak to his mother, and his request was granted. As the mother entered the room, he asked her to come closer because he wanted to whisper something in her ear. As she leaned towards her son, he tried to bite off her ear. Everyone was astonished, and when they asked him why he did that, he said that he wanted to punish her for not disciplining him when he was a child. He said, "Whenever I stole something, she would laugh and say, 'Nobody is going to notice.' It's because of her that I am here today."

The story reminds me of an experience I had when I was in the third grade. That year, our school had split sessions during the school day. My cousin Van and I attended the second session and would always go to the store around the corner before going to school. Everyday, though, we would meet this older girl, and she would take our treats. One day, I told Van that I was going back to get what I had bought from the store, and she wanted to know how. I said, "I'm going to steal it!" We went back to the store, and as Van watched, I succeeded in taking what I had originally purchased. I tried to justify my actions by telling myself that I had already paid for it but that it had been taken from me by that girl.

Once I walked out of that store, I felt like I could conquer the world. I felt that since I didn't get caught, I could do just about anything. I also felt that if I could do this every day, it would be the answer to some of our money issues. I was so excited that I ran home and told my mama. Gigantic mistake! I really believe that if the child protection services–I don't even know if there was such an agency–had been on top of things that day, Mama would have spent some time in the pen! She took care of business and talked later. I will never forget that horrible day, but it saved me a lot of heartache in the days to come. Mama didn't think my stealing was cute or funny…and I knew I'd never steal again!

Abraham Lincoln said, "All that I am and all I ever hope to be, I owe to my mother." That's exactly how I feel about my life. I appreciate my mother caring enough for me and teaching me to grow up being honest and respectful of others' belongings. The Bible says in Proverbs 22:6, "Train up a child in the way that you would have him to go and when he is older, he will not depart from it." Be reminded that those same little kids who talk back to you, hit you, and use ugly words are going to be grownups that talk back to you, hit you and use ugly words. Then it won't be so cute anymore. So take the brakes off, and train up your child!

There are so many people that are willing to help you. They are willing to "draft" or to be your protector as you work toward your goal. They are waiting to bless your life, but you must put yourself in a position to show them that you are worthy. You, too, must be willing to draft for others. Take the brakes off, and help somebody else.

Chapter 8

Bank

"I can do all things through Christ which strengtheneth me."
~~Philippians 4:13 (KJV)

By now you've learned enough race car lingo to be dangerous, so now I'm going to throw another term your way. The word is "bank." When race car drivers use the word "bank," they are talking about the angle of the track. All race tracks slant inward to aid the drivers; however, some tracks are more banked than others, meaning some are more difficult to navigate than others.

The race is on! There's no one in the car but the driver, and although he's having a tough time out there, going up and down and round and round, he's still got to hang in there if he wants to win.

Regardless of our position in life, whether we feel that our conditions are fair or unfair, despite what obstacles we've had to face or who is there in our lives to help us along the way, we're ultimately out there on our own, and it's either "put up or shut up." At some point in your life, God will put you in such a difficult situation that you will have no choice but to cry out to Him. As you go around and around the track of life, you can rest assured that it is not going be easy. Whether the track banks a little or a lot, it's up to you to go around the obstacles and get to the finish line.

Throughout your life, there will be knocks, hard knocks, and that's when you've got to summon up that extra HOLY GHOST POWER. When the devil sees that you are trying to go to the next level in your life, he calls a meeting with all of the demons in hell to discuss you. He gives them an assignment to take you down and destroy everything and every vision that God has given you. If you are not equipped with the Word to fight your battle, you will get out there on your own and get knocked out, and nobody can help you–not even your mama, regardless of how much she loves you–and that's the truth! You have got to be prayed up because you need that extra covering. You may have investors for that perfect idea or project that will propel you forward, but without the Word in your heart, you are going to go through unnecessary pain and suffering that could have been avoided.

Yes, God has great plans for your life, but they can only truly be fulfilled if you follow His instructions. So if you have something in your life that you really want to do, pick up the Bible, follow the instructions, and tell Satan and his imps to bring it on! Race car drivers drive their cars with their whole body, not just their hands. Isn't that the way it should be with us as we navigate through life and apply God's Word? Not only should we just pick up the Bible with our hands and read it, we need to put on the whole armor of God, so that we can be protected from head to toe. Satan wants to beat you up, and he is serious about winning the battle. If you are not grounded in the Word and not protected by the blood of Jesus, you are in for the beating of your life.

Pressure motivates me. I love challenges and movers and shakers. I am easily annoyed with people who feel that their lot in life is all there is. If you are stuck in a position on the job, are you going to stay there all of your life? Or do you start to look for something better? If there is something that you want to purchase or a dream vacation that you want to take, do you say, "I can't afford it?" Or do you go and create an income in order to do the things that you want to do? I know that God wants us to do more in life than procreate and work. And I really believe that He will take you to different levels in your life if you have the desire to move. He has so many ways that you can be a blessing to His Kingdom, but it's up to you to pursue something more. Think big, and think bold. Be unstoppable and get ready for your blessings to pour in. One thing that I have learned just recently is that just when you think you've gone as far as you can, God will send people that you've never heard of to usher you into your calling.

My late husband Cliff was a basketball official, and he would wear a t-shirt that read, "When the game is on the line, give me the ball, 'cause I ain't scared!" I believe if we had this type of attitude, we would be able to accomplish 100 percent more than we could ever imagine. We are living far below our potential, and there are so many opportunities that we have missed out on because we didn't give everything we had, or we did something our way instead of God's way.

Baseball great Hank Aaron said, "I always kept swinging. Whether I was in a slump or feeling badly or having trouble off the field, the only thing to do was to keep swinging." I remember when Hank's homerun news was the talk of the world. What I remember most about this man was his humble attitude. I remember hearing him speak one day at a high school, and I think he mentioned himself only once or twice. He never gave himself the glory. Anyone could tell that he was a child of the King. When you have a humble attitude, God will promote you beyond your wildest dreams. Hank was known as a quiet superstar because during his career, he received very little publicity as a result of his personality. His type of personality is very pleasing to God. His humility shows that if you want to continue your journey in a most rewarding way, you don't need to raise your own flag for your own glory.

I also remember that there was much turmoil surrounding the possibility of Hank's breaking Babe Ruth's record, and so many threats on his life, but he kept on swinging. Yes, he could have given up and blamed God for the color of his skin, but he kept swinging, and on April 8, 1974, he broke Babe Ruth's record with 715 homeruns.

Again, Hank Aaron made his own success, didn't make excuses and didn't ask for any man's help. And guess what else? According to the coaches, Hank wasn't even holding the bat the right way; he had taught himself how to bat and was batting cross handed. A lot of people couldn't understand his success because his technique was wrong; his success just didn't make sense—but things don't have to make sense when God is involved. Have you ever looked at someone else's success and thought, "How did they do that? How did they get ahead of me? Why do they seem to get all of the breaks, and they don't even appear to deserve them?" They never go to church, and you never see them pray and sometimes they will even tell you off at the drop of a hat! None of that makes sense to you. But do you know what?

It could be because they have a good heart and are willing to listen to God with their heart. Remember, God knows our hearts. It's not up to you to judge whether or not a person deserves what he/she has. When you judge, you bring damnation onto yourself, and that will negate the things that God has planned for your life. Don't wonder about why they're successful; instead, be happy for them and support them, and perhaps some of their blessings will rub off on you.

Another success story that I would like to share with you is about my friend Ralph Boston. In 1960, Ralph received the gold medal at the Olympics when he broke Jesse Owens' record. Ralph grew up in Laurel, Mississippi. (Have you ever heard of Laurel, Mississippi!?!) As Ralph puts it, he saw some tough times back in Laurel, Mississippi. He picked cotton, plowed the fields, slopped hogs and was judged by the color of his skin in one of the most racist states in the United States. Yet, Ralph made it!

I met Ralph back in 1968 when I first went off to Tennessee State for Ed Temple's summer program. I was a little girl, and one day after a workout, I went under the tree and sat next to Ralph. He called me his little sister, and we talked until we both rested and then, started up again.

Ralph, a tall, gracious, humble man, never once mentioned that he was a world record-holder. I knew about Jesse Owens, and there was a lot of talk going on around the school about Ralph. But I never knew that I was sitting next to the man who broke Jesse's record.

When I told Ralph in 2004 that I had retired, we started keeping in touch from time to time. He lives a wonderful, relaxing life now, and he often jokes around with me saying, "Are you really retired?" I guess he just wanted to show me how the retired life was really supposed to be lived, so he invited Linda, Isabelle (also an Olympian), her husband Rev. Holston, and me to visit him. On seeing his grand residences (his beautifully decorated primary home and his home on St. Simons Island), I kept thinking, "No way! How can a man of such humble beginnings have all of this?" Seeing what Ralph had, anyone would have thought that he was born into money. Ralph entertained us in grand style and gave us the opportunity to walk around and look at his awards, including the gold medal that he received when he broke Owens' record.

Like Hank Aaron, Ralph is a world champion and in the record books; yet, he is humble and meek. He realizes that it is only by the grace of God that he has accomplished all that he has. His story teaches us that if you achieve success God's way, He will definitely give you a spirit of meekness. Then will come the gifts of peace and soul rest.

Everyone wants a piece of the American dream, and some of us try to acquire material things by any means necessary, and this might even include get-rich-quick schemes that supposedly will propel you to the top in a flash. However, there are no shortcuts to reaching your destination. Let me say this again. There are no shortcuts to success! Have you ever seen people who appeared to have it all? If you check closely, though, you might see that many times, the grass is not greener on the other side, especially if God was not involved in the so-called "success story." When you do things your way instead of God's way, there will always be a void in your life and in your relationships, so much so that you will not be able to enjoy anything that you have. God's way takes time, but God's way brings true success, true happiness, and true peace.

I've always heard to be careful with things that come too easily. I've been told that if it's not of God, you'll know. One way of knowing is that God will send you signs. His way of letting you know when you're getting off track or off course is by way of the Holy Spirit. When Jesus ascended to the heavens, he said, "I will not leave you comfortless." Yes, he gave us the Holy Spirit as our guide to lead us into the direction that he would have us to go.

When we ignore God's signs, we experience so many setbacks in life, and we blame Satan; but we, not Satan, may be the culprit because we ignored God's signs. In race car driving, flags are used to communicate with the drivers. If the drivers disregard the flags (the signs), total chaos might result. Following is a list of the flags used in racing. Once we know what they are, we can see how they relate to our lives.

Green Flag: This is the "go" flag; when it flies, the race is on.

Single Cross Flag: This flag is sort of a "traffic congestion relief" signal; it's an indication for racers to move over and permit a pass.

Black Flag: This is not the flag racers want to see. This one is terminal, and the racer who receives this signal must get off the track and stop.

Red Flag: This flag is used to stop the race and applies to every car on the track; just like a traffic signal, red means "stop."

Double Cross: The double cross (or X) flag is an indication that the race has reached the halfway point.

White Flag: This flag indicates that there is only one lap left in the race; when the white flag waves, it's time to "hang it all out" or "hang it all up."

Checkered Flag: This is the flag the race leader wants to see. It is also the flag that every racer would like to experience. It means the race is over, and the leader is the winner.

Relate these flags to your personal life. How many flags have your ignored?

When God waved that Green Flag, He was saying, "I want you to go ahead with that idea; that dream that I have birthed in you will make you billions."

When God waved that Single Cross Flag, He was saying, "You're bringing in too many people and losing focus. They are getting in the way of what I promised you. I didn't promise them, I promised you. So move on over and let them go on ahead so that I can focus on you and your dream. If you keep hanging around with them, I'll give them the blessing that was intended for you."

Have you seen the Black Flag in your life? When God waved the Black Flag, He was saying, "You're not listening. Are you forgetting that you can only do great things through Me? Do I have to cause something tragic to happen in your life before you can appreciate what I am doing for you?"

Perhaps that sign still wasn't enough, so our Heavenly Father had to wave the Red Flag. When God waved this one, He was saying, "Stop! We need to talk. I sent My Son to die for you on the cross. I gave the only Son that I had so that you could have life and have it more abundantly. I knew what you were capable of being even before I laid the foundations of the earth. You are My beloved child, and I want to bless your life, but you need to help yourself and listen to My voice. I have given you a free will to choose, and I will not force you. You can continue to go round and round in circles not having a purpose in life, or you can give Me all of yourself and I will order your steps. Remember, the decision is yours, but I want you to know that you are covered by the blood of Jesus, and I want you to win! Yes, I want you to get the VICTORY!"

When God waved the Double Cross Flag, He was saying, "You're halfway to your destination, so don't give up. Keep your eyes on Me and I will be with you all of the way. People didn't believe you. They wouldn't invest with you, but look at you now. The race is not over, so don't give up. You've still got to focus because you can easily lose your edge. I know you've been at it for a long time, but just hang in there just a little while longer because with every round, I am going to take you closer to the finish line. You are going to have some difficult days ahead but trust Me and keep the faith, and you will be guaranteed the victory. I am God and I can do anything."

Aren't you grateful God gives us strength at times when we want to give up? Not only will He be our strength, but, like the Loving Father He is, He will give us words of encouragement. He is your biggest advocate.

When God waved the White Flag, He was saying, "Push that pedal to the metal 'cause you're almost there. Show them what you've got, and smile about it. I know that you hear the noise in the stands, but don't lose focus. Wait now, leave the applauding to the stands because if you start patting yourself on the back, I'm going to take My hand off you, and you will lose the race. Remember, you are moving ahead by My power, so keep your mind on Me. You're almost there. Picture yourself in the winner's circle. I want you to start practicing how you're going to receive that trophy when you cross that finish line. Practice what you're going to say when you walk across that stage because you will be the winner!"

When He waved the Checkered Flag, He was saying, "Congratulations! Make sure you always keep Philippians 4:13 tucked away in your heart—'I can do all things through Christ who strengthens me.'"

Through all of life's obstacles, you've got to believe in yourself. Rev up your gifts, and walk in faith, knowing that the Greater One is in you. Don't ever despair, regardless of what happens. Even if you crash into a brick wall and start spinning out of control, get back in the game. Whatever obstacles are thrown your way, remember that faith does not get you around trouble; it gets you through troubles.

Remember too that every trial does not come to destroy us. Trials develop patience and endurance, and that is how our character is formed. I know you know that the race does not always go to the swift, but to those who hold out the longest. So I encourage you to have the type of spirit that won't give up when things go wrong. I used to wonder how cars in a race that started out in the back eventually worked their way to the front and vice versa.

Then I realized that they have to take pit stops because of certain obstacles, and particular pit stops take longer than others. This is how we are in our lives. We all encounter difficult situations, but we each handle them differently, and that makes all the difference. God will give you everything that you need to overcome every obstacle in your life, but you have got to help yourself. Then and only then will you become VICTORIOUS!

Below are a few more suggestions on how you can live a victorious life.

Give Attention to the Things that Have Your Attention

Someone once said, "If you don't give attention to what has your attention at the time, it will take more of your attention than what it deserves." There are so many things to do and not enough time in the day to do them all, but we can't give up because life must go on.

When should you have made that deposit or balanced that bank book? When was the last time that you forgot to put that bill in the mail and had to waste time standing in line or paying the late charge? When are you going to have that heart-to-heart talk with your supervisor or co-worker? Instead of taking the time to do what you need, you spend hours and hours of sleepless nights because you have not handled your business. If you do not handle your business, though, it will definitely handle you, and it will not be as gentle. By doing the things that you should do when you need to do them, you can avoid a lot of problems down the road. Your life is meant to be more relaxing, and it can be if you take the brakes off and give attention to the things that have your attention at the time!

Walk It Out

We all know that walking is one of the best ways to keep a healthy body and mind. It also connects us to God and the spirit world. Have you ever strolled through the park or around the neighborhood observing all of the wonderful things in nature? The next time you go outside, leave the headset at home. Instead, enjoy the chirping sounds of the birds and insects. Take this time to praise God and thank Him for His wonderful masterpiece of nature. As you walk, stretch your limbs. Give Him glory for the strength to put one foot before the other. There are some people that have been in a wheel chair from birth and don't know what it is like to walk. They would probably give any amount of money if they could purchase the gift of health which would allow them to walk.

Your best investment is not in the stock market; it's in your health. Walking is healthy and can clear the mind; it is also good medicine for depression and helps with problem-solving. As you walk, ask God to allow thoughts to come into your mind that will point you to your destiny. So, the next time you want to work your body and lift your spirits, take the brakes off and walk it out!

Slow Down

Take care of yourself, and this includes getting enough rest, which, like walking, can benefit you physically and mentally. Take that much needed vacation or the personal leave that you deserve. A lot of times we feel that the office cannot get along without us. NEWS FLASH! If something happened to you today, you will be replaced tomorrow!

Take Richard Pryor's advice, "Hey man, slow that car down, this is a neighborhood; this ain't no residential district." So take the brakes off, and slow that car down!

Celebrate Yourself

Don't wait for a special occasion or someone else to celebrate you. Celebrate yourself! If you wait on others to celebrate you, you'll miss out on a lot of things that you want to do but don't because you're wishing you had someone to join you. Do it by yourself! When is the last time you passed up an event because you couldn't find a date? Go it solo sometimes and enjoy your own company because you're worth it. Likewise, don't wait around for others to validate you. If you want to run for office and no one will nominate you, what rule says that you can't nominate yourself. I did that one time and won. Cool, huh?

While you can easily celebrate yourself alone, sometimes you need to involve others. In today's society, everyone is ripping and running, and they may not see you for months at a time, even though you know that they love you and are concerned about you and what's going on in your life. However, have you ever been in the hospital for a period of time and no one came to see you? As you walked around the hospital and saw everyone else's room filled with balloons, flowers and cards, you wished that someone cared enough about you to at least make a phone call. Guess what? You might not have gotten anything because nobody knew that you were there! I can't believe the number of times that I have called to check on a friend and had them tell me that they had been in the hospital, but I never knew it until then. So the next time you are admitted to the hospital, have some type of system in place so that your friends can be notified. If people know that you are hospitalized, you will be surprised at the prayers and support you will receive to lift your spirit and help you to recover much quicker. And remember, if no one sends flowers, send your own.

Another way that you can celebrate yourself is to entertain yourself, not depending on others to join you. Many years ago, my girlfriend and I were on a cruise ship, and we visited a club where everybody was laughing, dancing and having lots of fun. There were several men sitting around checking things out, and I guess they thought that we were going to just either sit around or ask them to dance. I said, "Linda, I'm going on the dance floor. You wanna go with me?" She did. We had so much fun dancing by ourselves that afterwards, those same men asked us to dance to the next few songs. If you have a carefree, fun-loving attitude, you won't be by yourself long; your spirit will draw people to you. So take the brakes off and celebrate yourself!

Create Memories

When it's all said and done and you've taken your last bow, what can you sit back and reflect upon that will put a smile on your face? What about Sunday dinner with your children and grandchildren? What about scrapbooks, DVDs, going to the park, walking in the rain, or having friends over for movie night?

I love making memories. One memory that I have in my heart is having family dinner and my grandkids going outside and finding a pile of eggs under the house. Having fun, they started using the eggs like softballs, throwing them against the chestnut tree. Of course, with each egg they burst, I saw scrambled eggs, pound cakes, cornbread and every other delicious dish that called for fresh eggs. However, memories of them having fun like that are precious to me because they are very rare.

A tangible memory I've created is this: I have bought a birdhouse for each grandchild. The houses have their name on it and are in descending order, according to their age. I have also named my farm "Victoria's Farm and Tarance's Too," and I've purchased custom made street signs that say "Terra Boulevard" and "Thomi's Way" that I put on the drive leading to my back door. I've also created "Elizabeth's Garden" and named my cottage "William and Tyler's Juke Joint." Finally, I've created a file for each of my grandchildren. I put in things that they bring to me from school or church, including pictures and birthday invitations. When the past Presidential election was making history, I wrote each of my grandkids a letter announcing what was going on and indicating how old each was during this election, and I purchased a newspaper for each child to put in his or her folder. I long for the day when my grandkids gather around the table and share with their own children the good times that they had at Mema's house.

So whatever you do, take the brakes off and give yourself something that will bring joy to your heart years down the road. Despite the "bank" of the track of our lives, there are so many things that we can do to come out victoriously. Listening to the Holy Spirit is our biggest reminder when we are off course. If you want to live a life full of peace and contentment, take the brakes off, and listen to that inner voice.

Chapter 9

Silly Season

"Wisdom is the principal thing; therefore get wisdom; and with all thy getting get understanding."
~~Proverbs 4:7

The last term that I would like to share with you that is used by race car drivers is "silly season." When a race car driver's season is coming to an end, the team, after assessing itself, may make drastic, uncharacteristic changes, such as taking on new sponsors and hiring and firing drivers. Such a reassessment may also be necessary in our own lives. In order to move forward, you must be sure to have the best people in place in order to get the job done—people who will share your dream and support your vision. God wants you to be a winner, and although He has a plan for your life, sometimes you can abort your dreams by having the wrong people on your team or having team members who are out of position.

When there is someone on your team whom you feel is not producing, it doesn't mean that the person is useless, but rather that he/she may not be serving well in that particular position. Sometimes you may need to make adjustments. But remember, unless people know your expectations, your vision and plans are useless to all involved because everybody on your team should have the same goal. Someone once said, "If things get worse, I will have to ask you to stop helping me." Sounds funny, but it's true.

The same type of assessment can relate to family, friends and anyone who comes into your life. When someone enters your life and leaves you feeling terrible, regardless of the smiles and flattery, it may be a signal to let them go and move on. In this case, good and bad cannot occupy the same space at the same time. People are either for you or against you. You need to be able to distinguish the two. Always remember that it does not matter how good you are; it's your team and those with whom you surround yourself that will determine your success.

Have you ever been in a group where you have one or more persons who seem to major in being negative, who see the bad in everything? Those same people are the first at every meeting and will eagerly rip your plans apart. They always disagree, which is all right, but they are never ready with any suggestions or resolutions to make the situation better. There have been so many projects that have been shot down by one negative vote, resulting in dreams destroyed and hearts discouraged. Know that there will always be someone in the group who will doubt you, someone to always second guess you, and someone to undermine your authority; you must be careful about the position they have on your team; you can't ever put them in charge, or nothing will get done.

It is so very important that people, especially couples, work together for one common goal. I saw this epitomized when I went to a business anointing meeting on New Year's Day at the Ark of Salvation in Atlanta. The Pastor, Nathaniel Bronner, Jr., and his brothers anointed the business owners, and their mother anointed the spouses. When I registered for the meeting, I read the information on the website to get a better understanding of what would be happening. One thing that caught my eye was the letter that Nathaniel's mother wrote as she prepared for the meeting. She said that, as she was in prayer about what to say over the spouses, the statement that her husband spoke to her before marriage came to mind. She said that he told her, "If I have one person to think, to do, and to believe as I believe, there will be nothing impossible for us to achieve." Because that couple was of one mind, they went on to build one of the largest hair product empires in the world and became multi-millionaires.

God wants us to be more than conquerors. He wants us to be daring, fearless, creative and progressive. He wants projects that we take on to be professional and first class. Don't be afraid to shake up things with people who are in your group, but do it for the sake of progress. This should not only be in the office, club organizations or the church, but in your personal life as well. Let me restate that by saying, "Watch who you associate with." People are good, and people are wonderful; but people will hold you back. Instead of hanging with people all the time, keep a portfolio of friends, family and newcomers and have a meet-and-greet maybe once a year. Then you can catch up on the chit chat and small talk. This is what my girlfriend Dianne does. She's a mover and shaker and doesn't have time for a whole lot of small talk. However, Dianne will get like-minded people together periodically, provide a delicious meal, and let us take it from there. We don't hang around with each other otherwise, but we always have a wonderful time with her.

I don't have a lot of visitors, and I cannot think of anyone that I hang out with; however, I, like Dianne, know the value of getting together occasionally. When I celebrated my fiftieth birthday, my guest book signed in three hundred people, and all were friends and family.

Have you ever seen some people who cannot make a single move without having someone else tag along? I am not talking about true friend relationships. I'm talking about people who are afraid to be alone. If you have a friend that you trust and you have the time to spend with that person, you are blessed! However, being afraid to be alone is no reason to always have someone with you. That could be one reason that you are missing your blessings. Maybe God wants to bless you, but you may have "Gossiping Sally" always with you. It may be that the girl doesn't really like you, and if the truth be told, you really don't like her, but you are in a rut and used to tolerating the situation.

What happened here? I think we can analyze this situation by examining how you would cook a live frog. To cook a live frog, you would boil a pot of hot water, then throw the frog in. Immediately, you would see him hop out. However, if you put the frog in water at room temperature then turned up the heat very slowly, the frog will cook even before he realizes what has happened to him. It's because he'd gotten all warm and comfy. Like the frog you may have gotten comfortable with your situation, but that can be dangerous because comfort is an arch enemy of progress.

The next time you're out in a restaurant, observe other people around you. Most times, if you observe a bunch of women together, you can see the tension as they try to upstage one another. Watching them is really entertaining. Those same women probably gossip about each other, try to out-dress each other, and try to compete with each other for the attention of the men that come into the restaurant. Again, what has happened here is that these women have gotten used to hanging out together, and even though they may realize that they've outgrown each other, they are miserable but comfortable.

Relationships are wonderful, but they need to be kept in perspective. God put us on this earth for relationships, but we need to know which relationships are good for us and which ones are holding us back from reaching our dreams. When you share your dreams, which friends and family members applaud you, and which ones continue talking as if they didn't hear you?

Yes, we should avoid people who are holding us back, but we also need to realize that there are some people in our lives who are not out to get us. God will not always give us the people we want in our lives. When He puts a dream in our heart, He will also give us the people we need to help us realize that dream. When you have assessed your team, make sure that you don't get rid of the wrong people. Sometimes, the person who seems negative or intimidating may have been placed with you to help you see more clearly where you are going. For that reason, don't necessarily get rid of someone because you are intimidated, thinking he or she is smarter than you or has more experience than you. You need those people on your team. Team up with friends and family who will not be afraid to disagree with you or tell you when you're wrong or have messed up, those who will tell you the truth about yourself so that you can become a better person. If you have someone in your life whom you know has your best interest at heart, accept the truth they give in love.

In the sections that follow, I will share even more words of wisdom to help you navigate through the "silly seasons" of life.

Clear The Clutter

In order to make progress, we must clear the clutter in our homes. Just look around and see how much "stuff" could be going to those in need. When you go into those closets and storage areas, you will be surprised at the number of things that you will never use. Why are you hanging onto those things? Is it because of their sentimental value, or do you think you may need them down the road? Perhaps what you're holding onto can cause you to have negative emotions. What about that teddy bear that your ex gave you? What about the letter that's in your memory box announcing that you did not qualify for the job? What about that junk car that's an eyesore in the neighborhood? If you feel that you can't get on with your life, it may be because you are holding on to too much junk. If you have a storage house outside of your own place, you likely have more "stuff" than what you need. Loosen up and live the simple, carefree life that God intended. Get rid of the things that you do not want so that God will allow new and better things to enter into your life. So take the brakes off and remember, "You cannot give without receiving." That's God's law, not mine.

Clear the Mental Clutter, Too

Someone said, "If the horse has been dead for ten years, it's time to dismount." I say, "If the horse has been sick for one year, it's time to dismount." Get on with your life. Remember God's promise for our length of days, so why spend time worrying about the things that we can't change. If you are hanging onto emotions or feelings that are unproductive, why? Don't let things like hurt, anger, and disagreements with family and friends over something that was said or done years ago keep you in bondage. Remember that every day is a new day. Let the past go, and move on.

Again, there is hope. Mental clutter is toxic, and it is useless to dwell on the things that you cannot change. Sam Cooke says it best in his song entitled, "Keep Moving On." I urge you to take the brakes off; vow to do just that and leave behind mental clutter.

Stop Making Assumptions and Get the Facts

Let's say that an unpleasant situation has arisen, and you don't quite know how it came about. Do you want to know the truth about it, or do you wish to continue to remain in darkness by making assumptions? Understand, things are not always as they appear. You need to ask questions and get to the bottom of the confusion and drama. You will find that when you no longer make assumptions, people will be able to trust your words because you will be operating in truth.

Sometimes, we make assumptions about simple things, but we shouldn't. Don't assume that someone you know deliberately walked past you without speaking. Maybe that person didn't see you. Furthermore, don't assume that someone is upset with you because he/she hasn't called in some time or never sends you emails. The problem with people who make assumptions is that they feel people think and judge things the same as they do, and too often, they jump to negative conclusions.

For example, years ago I heard a young lady say, "No one likes me but men and children; everybody else is jealous of me." I was embarrassed for her for making such a senseless statement. I neglected to ask why she felt that way because, in my mind, some things do not need to be commented on. I am sure that you can plainly see who had the problem. Rather than assume that her statement was "senseless," I needed to have probed to find out the reason she said what she did. Making assumptions is like lies of poison because it keeps confusion going and keeps you from living the good life that God intended.

Another case in which I made an assumption happened to me about two months ago. I love to cook and love vegetables. I cooked some greens one evening, and when I sat down for dinner, I noticed that they were gritty. I was horrified because that had never happened before; I assumed that I had not washed the greens well enough, so I threw them away. The next day, I cooked cabbage, sat down to eat, and again, the same thing. I still couldn't figure out what was going on, and I was very disturbed. A couple of days later, I sprinkled salt on a tomato, and when I felt the grit, it hit me. It was the sea salt that I had been using in the vegetables that caused the grit. My point is this: suppose I had served these vegetables to guests at one of my meals and they also had the same experience that I had. The conclusion they might have formed was the same one I did at first—i.e., that I did not clean my vegetables. Had they made such an assumption, it could have hurt our relationship or even ruined my reputation. Making assumptions can be very dangerous.

Yet another incident is one that may have caused me millions. I was involved in an accident years ago, and I wanted a trial by jury. We were in court for five days, and during that time I felt comfortable with everyone on the panel with the exception of one lady. She never smiled at me like the others. She stared at me constantly and took plenty of notes and made me feel uncomfortable. However, there was a man that was exceptionally friendly. Each night my prayer was that everyone would go with the man and against the lady that I assumed had it out for me. At the end of the week the jury gave their verdict. Later, much to my surprise, I found out that the lady wanted to award me a million dollars, and the gentleman that I thought was really on my side found some kind of rule that denied that amount.

Sometimes I think about how I prayed against the lady and for the man. God answers prayer, so now I really know that we need to be careful what we pray for. The human mind does not know what's best for us so we really need to ask for guidance and wisdom more than anything else. Again, take the brakes off and stop making assumptions.

This Too Shall Pass

We all know that misfortune is a part of the human experience, but we can't let it steal our joy or make us bitter. Always remember that weeping may endure for a night, but joy comes in the morning. Sometimes people are so hurt over situations that they dare not forget and won't let you forget either. God is our Comforter, and He is the one who handles negative situations for us. When we take it upon ourselves to get revenge on those who have hurt us, that's when we mess it up.

I am not suggesting that you forget about pain or hurt or set it aside completely; however, I am saying don't let Satan use you. If you do, he will win and cause you to miss out on the blessings that God has in store for you. Whenever you worry, become fearful, or hang onto painful experiences, you're prolonging the situation and missing out on a wonderful life. As long as we're trying to deal with the problem, God will not move. He will not come to our rescue until we lay it down and hand it over to Him.

Then, and only then, will He change the situation to work out for the good. Just trust Him.

Sometimes we don't know why we're going through the hurt and pain in our lives, but we need to realize that there is a reason for everything. Have you ever considered that God may be using your situation to make you stronger in your faith? Whatever you do, trust Him and know that your affliction is for a moment. You can probably think of negative experiences in your life which almost broke you, but you're still here and you're much better because of those situations. Keep the faith and watch God work miracles in your life! Go ahead, take the brakes off, and don't let your past destroy your present!

<u>Where Is Your Faith?</u>

There are so many times in life when we all want to throw in the towel, but know that God's Word is truth. We are commanded to travel this road based on what we have believed in our hearts that God will do, instead of what we see with the naked eye. In order for our faith to be strengthened, we must take it upon ourselves to study. There are so many good things that God has prepared for us, but so many times, we miss out because we don't know the Word. How can we believe if we don't know what to believe?

I remember taking my daughter Terra to the hospital for major surgery when she was three years of age. She had swallowed the back part of an earring, and it was lodged inside of her lungs. The doctor came up to the room with the X-ray and showed her dad and me the picture and explained to us that she needed a very serious operation because the particle was lodged in the alveoli in an awkward position. When the doctors went out of the room, we prayed and asked God if He would be the doctor that day and guide the surgeon's hands. The team came up to roll Terra into the operating room, and within 10 minutes she was back with no surgery needed. The doctor showed us the X-rays, and the item had disappeared!

God cares for us so much that He has assigned angels to each one of us to carry out our requests, and that's no fairytale. Read your Bible because it's in the Word. So if you really want to please God, take the brakes off and trust that He will do just what He said He would do.

Yes, always remember that God wants us to live our best lives and if we are to do so, we must take time and evaluate our situation and make some hard decisions; this might result in a "silly season" for us. However, until we make a concerted effort and ask God to help us make the right decisions and to change the situation, we will not make much progress. Yes, take the brakes off, and know that with God's help, you can do anything.

Chapter 10

Follow the Road Map

"This is what the LORD says— your Redeemer, the Holy One of Israel: I am the LORD your God, who teaches you what is best for you, who directs you in the way you should go."
~~Isaiah 48:17 (NIV)

Whew! You've been on the best ride ever, and I hope that you have learned enough about how to maneuver through life in order to get you to your final destination.

Sometimes we set out for a road trip with no direction, having no road map, no GPS and sometimes, no idea as to where we want to go. We go in circles and waste a lot of time. Then sometimes, after we've been traveling wherever for a while and are almost where we think we want to go, we give up and turn back because we think that we're lost.

Sometimes the same thing happens to us on our Christian journey—that is, we are not sure where we are going. Like I mentioned earlier, I heard a minister on television speaking, and he gave me something to think about. His question to the listening audience was "How do you really know that there's a God?" My first reaction was

"Everybody knows that!" Then he explained the question a little more when he said, "What I am asking is this: other than your parents making you go to church or your taking the kids to Sunday school or what others have told you, what personal experience have you had to prove that there is a divine, supreme being in the universe?" That was the very first day that I made a personal decision to search for the truth myself.

Although I had experienced the presence of God in my life at an early age, my answer to the minister's question was based on the fact that I was raised in the church and baptized at the young age of twelve. I went on church trips, said Easter speeches and sang in the choir. We had church picnics and sold candy for the building fund. (Interestingly enough, when I went back to my home church in 2009, I observed that we still do not have a new building. Sometimes I wonder if it's because, like me, most people ate all of the candy and didn't pay for it! Remember, I was a kid.) Because my mom and the preacher told me that there was a God, I thought that He was all of the above: church picnics, Easter speeches, selling candy and being baptized.

However, as I study the scriptures and look back over my life and see how He has revealed Himself to me, I know that there is a higher power, and I choose to call that higher power God. I read a lot, and as I relate what I read to the scriptures and look at my past and present and concentrate on my future, I know that there's a force out there that cannot be reckoned with. To me, it doesn't matter what man believes. It only matters what God has said in His word and has demonstrated time and time again in the lives of believers. My question to you is this: how do you know that there's a God?

The basis of Christian belief is the Holy Bible, and, as such, I believe that the Bible should be our road map as we travel the Christian journey. Some people look at the Bible as merely a book written by men; however, the Bible is the final authority on how we must live our life. But until you have had a divine intervention from Heaven, you may not be able to recognize this fact. No one should ever believe because someone wants him to believe; rather, everyone must be convinced on his/her own. That's why it is very important that we have our own personal relationship with God, our Heavenly Father.

A result of that relationship is our acceptance of God's salvation. Being saved does not mean that you're going to start being perfect all of a sudden. What it does mean is that you have invited God into your heart, and you are willing to follow what is required of you to be like His Son. Some people feel unworthy of salvation because their schedule will not allow them to attend church on Sundays or they don't have money to tithe or do other things expected of church members. However, when you accept Christ into your life, He will make it so you can eventually do what you need to, to honor Him regardless of what you have. Then, blessings will start to overflow into your life, and He will open the windows to Heaven so that you won't have enough room to receive them all. I am not telling you to seek salvation in order to get more "things"; I'm saying to do these things because you love Him and He loves you.

Other people feel that they are not worthy because of their character. Well, neither is Sister Lucy who just got off the dance floor at 2:00 this morning. Neither is Deacon Charlie who's still on probation for child support. What about the Pastor who's having some questionable thoughts about the choir director? God is definitely not pleased with their behavior, and eventually, these people, along with all of us, will have to give an account for our disobedience. So don't ever think that you are not worthy of being in His house. God loves everybody and I sincerely and prayerfully hope that you realize that it's important to be surrounded by other people who, like you, are trying to be more like Christ. Yes, there are hypocrites in the church, and some of us are turned off by their behavior. But there is much more in the house; there's love in the house, there's fellowship in the house, and there's protection in the house. And this is one place you can come as you are.

I was told that, when I was a child, I was bad. However, when I look back over my life, the kinds of things I used to do then, compared to what is going on in the world today, I can't see where I was so bad. My biggest problem came from trying to take up for everybody. I didn't even have to know a person to stand up for him/her if I thought that he/she were being taken advantage of—and I'm still like that today. In my attempts to protect others, though, I don't remember getting into many fights because I would always be the first one to throw a punch, then I would run. That was my specialty—do unto others before they did unto me. This sometimes caused me problems because I sometimes forgot that once I did the hitting and ran inside the house, I had to go back outside eventually.

Sometimes I'd have to hide out all day, ruining the rest of my day. Here I would be, looking out of the window and seeing everyone else outside playing and having fun, even the person that I had taken up for. That person wouldn't even come inside and play with me! I'd stare out of the window, then go and look at TV, then look out of the window some more. And every time I looked out, the person I had hit would be standing outside with his (it was always a boy) fist balled up saying, "Come on out of the house." Of course, I didn't go out. After that wouldn't work, he'd start talking about my mama and my family and trying to remind me of what happened to me the last time I tried to take up for somebody.

He'd talk really big just to get me out of the house. Sometimes, some of the other kids would come knocking on my door (including the kid that I had taken up for) trying to trick me into coming outside so that I could get beat up. I still kept my distance, though. As the day passed, the kid with the balled up fist would finally say, "Okay, Loretta, we can be friends. Just come out on the porch. I'm not going to bother you." But that still wasn't enough to convince me. I would stay in the house for days until, tired of being cooped up, I finally went back outside and got what was coming to me. When that happened, I became part of the group again.

The biggest fear that I had was leaving the house, and that's the same way I want you to feel about leaving the house of God. Satan is telling you, "Come on out. I'm not going to bother you. Remember what happened the last time? Man, you almost had it all." That's right. The devil is whispering in your ear, "Stop looking out of the window and come on the front porch so that we can have some fun. I hope you forgot about the last time that we met up." Well, you do remember the last time, but you also remember you escaped the enemy because somebody, probably your mother, was praying for you. (Thank God for praying saints!)

Still, what Satan wants to do is pull you away from other believers so that He can have a better chance at destroying you and your family. He will use any tactic to get you out of the house, but God's promise of salvation is all you need to protect you.

Sadly, there are people who feel that they have no need for God's salvation. As long as they are going about their lives with friends, good jobs, health, and money in the bank, they think they're fine. If this is you, I want you to know that there will come a time when these things will not be important, and your heart will not be able to find any rest until you develop a relationship with your Heavenly Father. Do understand that being a member of the church is not the same as being saved. Neither does being saved mean that you are no longer a sinner. We will always be sinners, but remember that Jesus died and rose on the third day so that he could be an intercessor for us sinners.

I want to share a poem with you entitled *"He's Coming Back Again"* by Diana Byrd, author *of Love Is Straight from the Heart,* about the coming of our Savior.

He's Coming Back Again

He's coming back again, and it will be sometime soon,
No one knows whether it will be in the morning or at noon.
Make sure you're ready to meet your Maker at this time so
you won't be committed for an eternal crime.

He's coming back for those who obeyed the golden rules,
But to those who didn't, their lives they will lose.

Of course you still have to get your life intact,
But you better not take too long, 'cause He's coming back.

There are some who go to church to show off their pretty clothes,
Your pastor, family, and friends may not know who you are,
But the Lord knows.
Fine clothes, fine cars, and money won't get you on His train,
So get your life together, 'cause He's coming back again.

Don't take my word for it, just read the good book,
And just like me, you too will also get hooked.
This can be a fresh start and not a bad end.
Get your life in order, 'cause He's coming back again.

For all of you nonbelievers out there, let me break it down to you this way. I would rather believe that there's a God and find out that there is not one when I die than to not believe, die and find out that there is one!

In this chapter we discussed believing in God, what it means to be saved, and using the Bible as a road map to guide you through life. I want to end this book with still more insights about how you can prepare yourself to navigate the road of life.

Act Like a Child

The Bible says in Matthew 18:3, "Verily I say unto you, except ye be converted, and become as little children, ye shall not enter into the kingdom of heaven." If you have children or if you're ever around children, you'll notice how happy and carefree they are. They are totally dependent on their parents, whom they love unconditionally, and they love their friends and siblings without a second thought. Yes, they have little fights, but they don't carry around hurt and attitudes that we as adults do. If we can let up off the brakes and go forward showing unconditional love, forgiveness, kindness and compassion toward others, we will hear from God and reap the harvest that He has in store for us. So take the brakes off, and act like a child!

Laugh Your Way Out

Don't be so serious about life. Laugh for the sake of laughing. Laughter is like medicine to the soul. Place your trust in God, and you will have all the reason in the world to laugh and be happy. God will give you a genuine spirit of joy and peace. Even when others are around trying to figure out "what's the point," laugh anyway. Moreover, expect others to laugh. Even if you're not the playful type, try not to snuff out the flames of others who are and who take great pleasure in making others laugh.

Some people have a knack for making others laugh. My cousin Jerrold was one such person. He kept the whole family on edge all of the time with his jokes. He was always the life of our family gatherings, and he always kept spirits up. He always had the whole family laughing with his antics.

Another person is my grandson, Tyler. He takes some really cute and funny pictures. I've put one of those humorous pictures over my bed so when I wake up in the morning, I will have something to laugh about. Before retiring to bed at night, I sometimes just look at his picture and burst out laughing.

I love playing with all of my grandchildren. I remember one day while they were visiting me that it started to rain. First I considered calling them inside, but then I decided to go outside with them and join in the fun. We started laughing and playing and even I, a grandma, had loads of fun out there in the rain. Remember, people don't stop laughing because they grow old; they grow old because they stop laughing. So take the brakes off, lighten up, have fun with life and start laughing!

Take Charge of Your Own Health

You are only as good as your health will allow you to be. How's your health? Regardless of who you are or what you have, you cannot accomplish anything without good health. You will be a tremendous blessing to the Kingdom when your health is at its best.

For that reason, you must take charge of your health and be proactive. Statistics show that for every dollar that we spend being proactive, we spend thirty-six dollars down the road because we were not proactive. If you want a good life and want to be around in years to come so that you can enjoy your grandchildren, you might need to rethink your health choices. You might say to yourself that there is not much you can do now since taking care of yourself was not a priority in the past...that the toothpaste has left the tube and we can't put it back. However, you can make a vow to take care of your body from here on out.

One thing you should do is be aware of what might be in your food and clothing without your knowing it. Try going to the Internet and google the words "chlorine bleach," "arsenic," and "formaldehyde" in their relationship to what you eat and what you put on your body. What you'll find will frighten you. Did you know that chlorine bleach is actually used on fruits and fish to give them that fresh, clean appearance? No wonder some of us feel sick and tired all of the time! So when you pride yourself on eating only fish or chicken, you are not eating as well as you thought.

In considering your health, be very careful with the people that you trust in the medical field. Although we rely on products regulated by the FDA, you need to take it upon yourselves to do your own research when your health is involved. Don't trust medical doctors to have your best interest at heart; rather, trust your body and your feelings. Just because you are prescribed certain medications does not necessarily mean that the medicine is good for you. Read about the side effects on the label; you might find that you are better off with your illness as opposed to what might happen if you take the medication. When a doctor gives you drug samples, these are samples given by salesmen in an attempt to get the office to purchase their line of products. No one is just being nice to you; they are trying to make money, and the more they sell, the more money they make. Don't be their guinea pig.

In addition, you need to remember that not all doctors are authentic, and some real doctors don't have your best interest at heart. They may prescribe medications without taking time to see you, or they may order tests and procedures that you don't need. These are ways that they can just get your money. So, the next time you set your foot into a healthcare facility or a doctor's office, make sure you've done your research by finding out a bit about them first. There are Internet sites that will tell you about the doctor's background in general, and others can tell if there have been any lawsuits or claims filed against the doctor in question. There are so many resources to assist you, and doing your research can save you thousands of dollars and a whole lot of heartache and pain.

There are other things, too, that you should be aware of. When in the doctor's office, observe the attitude of the staff or other workers. If necessary, start up a conversation with other patients waiting to be seen by the doctor. See how many people are on the doctor's staff. Look around to see how the office is kept, and notice whether or not the equipment and tools are clean. Try to hold enough of a conversation with the doctor to observe his/her temperament and level of experience. If there is any uneasiness (that is, if that little voice inside tells you all is not right), you should leave because your health may be at stake.

I am reminded of a time when my daughter Terra, who had bit down on an olive seed and cracked her back tooth, was referred to a particular dentist to get a root canal. I had a long talk with her and warned her of the types of things to look for since she did not know this dentist. Later that day, she called me back to share her experience about her dental visit. She told me that after she was medicated, she was informed that the wait time for the tooth to become numb would be about twenty minutes. The assistant allowed her to sit up in the chair, and as she looked around the room, she observed instruments lying on a bare counter that did not appear to be clean. Rather than have the procedure done, she decided to get out of there.

I also remember the mother of one of my friends. One evening, that friend Quincy brought his mother, Ms. Annie, over to pick up a gift basket. Ms. Annie was visiting from out of town, and it was my first time meeting her. She was a nice, sweet lady and in a wheel chair, and her speech was impaired. I asked Quincy about the situation, and he explained to me that she had taken a prescription medicine that had been recalled, but not before the medicine had wreaked havoc on her health.

Further, I was in a class years ago when a former doctor told the entire class that she could not count the number of times that she had performed open heart surgery while being high on crack. Devastating isn't it? But I know that she is not the only one to have done that same thing.

Much of what I've said so far relates to physical health. However, emotional health is just as important. Do you know how harmful negative emotions can be? You cannot afford the luxury of a negative thought. Negativity counteracts everything that you are trying to do with your health. Being negative or being around negative people who are always complaining and trying to find something to argue about can have devastating effects. Negativity causes heart attacks, strokes, cancer, high blood pressure, and many other similarly serious diseases. As you avoid what's negative, why not take a special effort to spread positive attitudes. If you are upbeat, your physical health will benefit. So take the brakes off, and take charge of your own health!

Dressed to The Nines

1 Peter 3:3-4 (NLT) says "Don't be concerned about the outward beauty or fancy hairstyles, expensive jewelry, or beautiful clothes. You should clothe yourselves instead with the beauty that comes from within, the unfading beauty of a gentle and quiet spirit, which is so precious to God." In today's society, we so often are judged by how we look and what we wear, but God looks at the heart. You were created for a purpose and when God made you, He made a masterpiece. You are His handiwork, and you are beautiful, so you want your outward appearance to reflect your inner beauty. Make sure you are always neat, clean, and attired appropriately. When you do that, regardless of how much your outfit cost, you'll be "dressed to the nines." So take the brakes off, and stay dressed to the nines! People are watching you.

Learn to Be Content and Happy

Father Alfred D'Souza, an inspirational writer and philosopher, once said, "For a long time it seemed to me that life—real life—was about to begin, but there were always some obstacles in the way: something to get through first, some unfinished business, time still to be served, and a debt to be paid. At last it dawned on me that these obstacles were my life. This perspective has helped me to see that there is no way to happiness. Happiness is the way. So treasure every moment you have and remember that time waits for no one. Happiness is a journey, not a destination."

Throughout this book, I have tried to offer you suggestions on ways that you most definitely can navigate through life on cruise control. You already have your road map because you have your Bible. However, along with the map, I've given you some landmarks. With the two, you should be able to progress on your Christian journey, achieve your goals in life, and be happy. What more could you want?

Epilogue

"For we are God's [own] handiwork (His workmanship), recreated in Christ Jesus, [born anew] that we may do those good works which God predestined (planned beforehand) for us [taking paths which He prepared ahead of time], that we should walk in them [living the good life which He prearranged and made ready for us to live]."
~~Ephesians 2:10

    I would like to thank you for reading *Life Is Always in Progress...So Take the Brakes Off*. Now that you've read the book, I would like to share with you how the book came to be and what some of my inspirations were for making this work. As always, my inspiration comes from God as led by the Holy Spirit. He is the Alpha and the Omega, the beginning and the end. I believe that nothing in life happens before its time, and nothing happens by coincidence. Furthermore, I am convinced that God is trying to get our attention when we are burdened with the feeling that our life is going around in circles, even though we have more to offer but just can't seem to get it together.

    Has there ever been a time when you've said to yourself, "There's got to be more to life than this?" Or maybe you've thought, "I feel like there's more to me than what I'm doing. It feels as if I am not doing all that I know I can do, and I know that God wants more from me." It's almost like there's another life inside of your body and soul just waiting to make its grand entrance. And it seems like everywhere you turn, God is there to help you out. But with your busy schedule and fast-paced lifestyle, there's always something to do before you can really do exactly what you're called to do. For some reason, the timing is never right...but the fact remains the same: there's something going on inside of you that needs to happen.

As we all know, all of life is beautiful, but the one thing we cannot predict with exact accuracy is the actual birth—or should I say timing—of those moments that most define who we are. Of course, like everything else, we work hard, make big plans and wait, only to anticipate when and how our plans will turn out. On the other hand, there are some things that we set out to do, exerting very little human effort, yet, for some reason, everything that we touch, hear, breathe, see or taste related to those things turns to gold. It's almost like you say something or you have a fleeting thought and the angels grab it, take it back to the Master, and the rest is history. That's how *Life Is Always in Progress...So Take the Brakes Off* came into being. It was just a fleeting thought.

I want to share with you the making of this book, and as you follow along, I want to show how God was with me from the beginning–in my thoughts, ideas, suggestions and even simple things that others would probably consider a coincidence. God was with this project from day one.

As I think back over my life, I reminisce about the days when I taught high school. I was a Health and Physical Education instructor, and I really enjoyed being in the classroom. The best part about being in the classroom was that I had a listening audience, especially when students wanted to divert my attention away from giving them a test. On Fridays, my students were assigned to bring in current events articles, and most times, those articles turned into major lectures from me. It seems as if there was never enough time in the class period to complete my lessons, as those lessons would always go bell-to-bell.

One year, I had a student named Benny who rarely showed up for class. Benny was very quiet and observant, very smart, mature and laid back. Most of the time it appeared that Benny was in his own world, but I really didn't have an opportunity to get to know him because he was only in my class for a short time. One day as I was speaking to the class, much to my surprise, Benny raised his hand, and the entire class fell silent. You see, this was the first and only time that Benny had raised his hand for anything.

When I acknowledged Benny, he said, "Why don't you write a book?" To be sure that he wasn't trying to egg me on so that I could do more talking, I asked him why. Benny was very serious as he said, "You really have a lot to say, and maybe that's the way a lot of people can hear you." Then he went on to say, "If not a book, what about a talk show?" As smoothly as he made those suggestions, his disappearance was equally so. You see, Benny left without saying goodbye. For some reason, he never returned to class. That was almost two decades ago. To this day, Benny may not be aware of this, but he was the first person to plant the idea of putting my thoughts on paper. A little 15-year-old kid put something in my mind and spirit that has stayed with me until the exact time that it was supposed to be birthed.

Life is always in progress...so take the breaks off

We all know that our timing is not God's timing, and above all else, our plans are not God's plans. But when God gets ready to put something into action, He will shake up the entire universe, move across the highways and byways, cause rivers and oceans to stand at attention, open doors that no man has ever dared open, and not allow any door to be shut until it's time. And above all else, I know from experience that when it looks like the door is getting ready to close, He will push you inside right in the nick of time. I shudder in awe at the awesome power of God.

I retired from the DeKalb County School System in 2004, and I have been fortunate enough to enter into my second career as the CEO of Simply Blessed Gift Creations, a gift basket company. One day, as I was making a delivery to one of the high schools, a beautiful lady asked for a business card, and later on I started making deliveries to her home. I eventually learned that she was a writer, and she invited me to her book signing. That is when the spirit of God led me to finish a project that I started working on 17 years ago.

Years back, I can remember putting together notes, articles and pieces of information in hopes of one day writing a book. Although I had oftentimes talked about writing a book, it seems as if God put her in my presence at the right time to inspire me to do so. Although I am usually a procrastinator, once I made up my mind to do this project, God placed so many people in my life to inspire me and help me do what I basically had no desire to do on my own. I thank God for that.

Initially the title of my book was going to be *The Game Of Life Is Never Over Until the Final Whistle Has Blown*. The cover was really nice. It had a big stop watch and a whistle on it. I chose that name because years back, there was a sports announcer named Chico Renfroe who would come on station WIGO every Saturday morning and announce the high school game of the week, as well as the results of other sports contests. I listened to him every chance I got because I simply loved hearing my name called out on the radio. (I was a three-time state champion in Georgia in the 100 meters, and our track team won three state championships during that time.) After every sportscast, Mr. Renfroe would end his session with, "The game of life is never over 'til the final whistle has blown," and I just loved those words and the jingle that went along with it.

My first idea was to talk about my high school track team and teammates, my teammates at Tennessee State, and just about every type athlete that I could think of...dead or alive. I especially wanted to write about my good friend Ralph Boston because he's one of the most humble and generous athletes I know. Writing about athletes would have been so very easy since I had access to the living legends (including the Tigerbelles at Tennessee State), and our school was having our reunion in a couple of months. Nevertheless, something happened to make me change my mind about both the title and the contents of the book.

I had purchased a brand new sofa about eight months earlier, but it was accidentally ripped. Since I had insurance, I was told that I could go into the store for a trade of equal value. After walking around for more than an hour without finding anything to suit my taste, I finally went to the salesman and told him that I would check back at a later date. He informed me that I had only five days left to honor my contract, so rather than leave, I began searching desperately, going throughout the entire store, looking in corners and behind makeshift showcases, and praying to God to help me find something that would make me happy and get me out of that store.

Continuing my search, I noticed a really nice picture with a rooster; on it were etched these words: "Life Is Always In Progress." Instantly, I knew that was my book title because that saying made an unusual connection with my spirit. God is always in the blessing business, but sometimes He wants us to search, dig a little deeper, and not give up so easily. You see, just as I was getting ready to give up my search for the sofa, He revealed my blessing for something else. I believe that everything in life happens for a reason, and I truly believe that my sofa tear was God's way of helping me choose this title. Keep in mind that I had a lot of information on my original title, and I was set to go with it.

A second lesson from the sofa tear was that everything that seems bad is not necessarily so. I was really upset when the sofa was damaged, and I was even more upset because at first, I had not been able to find a new sofa that I liked. However, sometimes God will allow things to happen in your life in order for you to move on to the next level—and that is what the sofa experience did for me.

I was so excited about the wonderful piece of artwork that I bought it and took it home, then went to the Internet to check out the artist, Rodney White. I fell in love with his style of work. Although he now resides in New York, he is a self-taught artist who graduated from Dekalb Technical Institute, which is about five minutes from where I live. His work has a vintage style and depicts the lifestyle of a serene, calm, peaceful atmosphere. Since Rodney's picture had a rooster on it, I decided to take pictures of my rooster figurines and of a few live roosters to go along with my book. I wanted to create the same kind of good, easy, laid back type atmosphere, so I decided to also show pictures of my barn and cottage and of my llamas grazing in the pasture, the lazy cat sleeping on the back porch, and the grandkids playing in the field.

A few days passed, and although I was excited about the project, I felt that there was something missing. I knew that I wanted to portray a peaceful, relaxed feeling to my readers, but as I said earlier, the title and content did not capture what the Spirit was saying to my soul, and I couldn't figure it out. That night, I prayed about it, and I asked Him, "God, how do people really get to that point of surrender and just enjoy life? How do people really find their purpose in life, and how do they really find the peace that so many of us are searching for?" He spoke to my heart and said, "You will find your purpose in life and come to that peaceful place when you release anything that hinders you from being the best person that you can be and when you release anything that keeps you from fellowshipping with me."

Still not sure of my direction, I fell asleep that night. However, I awakened the next day with an "aha" moment as God whispered in my ear "So Take the Brakes Off!" I knew it! That was my subtitle! It would clearly tell my readers to release anything in their life that is keeping them from being the best person that they can be. Now I felt like I was making some progress, and that's when I actually realized that this book was God-inspired.

With my title decided upon, I didn't want the country look anymore because it did not match my book title. After all, chickens don't have brakes. (Smile) So I thought about what I wanted to do. When I thought of brakes, I thought of some type of race cars, but what would cars have to do with living a peaceful life? Much to my surprise, when I googled race car driving, I got lots of information for my book project, as there is terminology that race car drivers use, as I discussed throughout the book, which directly correlated to the things that we need to do to live a peaceful, abundant, God-filled life.

Now tell me that's not God! Like my grandbabies Victoria and Elizabeth always say after their prayers, "Hallelujah, praise the Lord!" I could not believe it. This was just too good to be true. I said to myself, "That's my book, and God did it all." But He didn't stop there.

After God gave me the book title and the book contents, I had another dilemma. The book cover had to change. As I mentioned previously, I pictured a big rooster, the barn, and an array of earth tone colors, but that didn't go well with the title or the content. Then I thought about a plain book cover with just the title. That was okay, but it still wouldn't do my book justice. Then God came through again!

One evening as I was preparing to go to my gift basket meeting, I was trying to find something to take as a covered dish. I had no reason to look in the back of the cabinet, but an inner voice kept saying, "Use what you've got." I opened the cabinet twice but didn't see anything to take to the meeting. However, something told me to go back and look a third time. I did, and in doing so, I moved every can out of the way and found, tucked back into the far right corner, an expired can of black-eyed peas with a black and white checkered background resembling a race track flag. Another "aha" moment! That was my book cover! But hold onto your seat because God's revelations to me didn't stop there.

There's a scripture that talks about how God's blessings will chase you down and overtake you, and that's what I confess happened to me during this book project. A couple of days later, while I was volunteering at a high school, Ms. Byrd, a Physical Education teacher and also a published author herself, walked into the classroom with checkered pants, the same design as my book cover, and a matching shirt. I couldn't believe my eyes. I gasped and declared, "That's my outfit when I do my book signings." No human being could have ever orchestrated the chain of events as such. Again, I am here to testify that this is most definitely God's project, and I am so thankful that He is using me to carry out this mission.

Everything that I have described above is proof positive that God is the mastermind of this project, and He has guided me every step of the way. I am most thankful that He used me as His vessel to deliver this message, and I am still baffled by all he revealed to me to get the project going.

I reiterate that the longer I live, the more I am convinced that nothing just happens. God was preparing me for this day through the series of seemingly unrelated occurrences. I say this because months before the inception of this book, I complained to my daughter Terra that I was awfully tired; in fact, some mornings it was very difficult for me to get out of bed. My entire body ached from head to toe, and I was just drained to the point where normal everyday tasks were difficult for me to perform. I found a homeopathic doctor who diagnosed my condition as fibromyalgia.

Fibromyalgia is a chronic condition that causes stiffness, pain and tenderness of the muscles. Sufferers have difficulty sleeping and, upon rising, feel tired and fatigued. The condition is really painful, and leaves you feeling overwhelmed by your physical limitations. Now who could take on any serious project under these conditions without the help of God? I knew—and know—though, that if God brings you to it, He will see you through it. When there is something in life that you really want to do, just make up your mind to do it, and God will handle the rest. I was determined to overcome my fibromyalgia.

Although I had been to the doctor, I was still up and down until one day my friend Johnny called and said, "Hey Lo, let me take you out to lunch." When he got to my house, I said, "Johnny, I feel terrible, almost like killing myself." Don't panic now. I know the power of the tongue, and I instantly rebuked those words even though I was joking around when I said them. Still, I really surprised my own self for making that statement, which Johnny took seriously. As we headed out, he said, "First let's stop off at my doctor's office to see if he can help with your condition." We went to what appeared to be a health food store which sold only natural products. As I walked around picking up different products, a nice young lady behind the counter informed me that I should not purchase anything until I could be seen by their doctor, who would have to perform muscle testing before recommending any products.

I was determined to get better, so I was back in the doctor's office the very next day for my first appointment—and I feel like a million bucks today! I don't know if I can compare my experience to Lazarus' being raised from the dead, but I really feel alive now. I can run, jump, and do most of the things that I did years back. My daughter Thomi gave me a membership to the Y.M.C.A., and I go every morning—treadmill, yoga, lifting, whatever…I just feel great! The scripture says, "Beloved, I wish above all things that thou mayest prosper and be in good health, even as thy soul prospereth" (3 John 1:2). I had no idea at the time that my overcoming fibromyalgia was the orchestration of God's divine power. But I realize now that He was really serious about helping me to fulfill this assignment and wanted me to be alert and well. What did I say earlier? If God brings you to it, He will see you through it.

Okay, now I was set to go. I'd gotten my idea for the book title, and my health was doing fine; but there was still a problem that I needed to overcome. The publisher told me to start advertising for my book signing by telling people what I was doing. I really didn't feel like talking to anyone about it. Oh, I mentioned it to both my daughters and my big sister Eunice, and they all complimented my efforts and encouraged me in the pursuit. But I really didn't share much about my plans at first.

Then, a few weeks passed, and I mentioned my project to my friend Gregory. The more I talked to him about this project, the more energized I became, like this was really going to happen for me. God left me with this one last message. "I will never give you anything that you cannot handle. I will send someone into your life to help you accomplish what I have purposed for you to do." Like Mama would always say, "People need people." God chose Gregory to help me carry out this mission.

At one point, I really became discouraged and decided to give up altogether. However, as soon as I called it quits, I met a wonderful woman (my BBF) by the name of Michelle who gave me encouragement each and every single day.

All said and done, I again say thank you, God, for putting situations, both good and bad, and people in my life that have had anything to do with the making of Life Is Always in Progress…So Take the Brakes Off.

Finally, I want to close by saying that I really hope you have enjoyed reading this book. Regardless of what message or information you've decided to allow the Holy Spirit to download inside of you, it is my sincere prayer that you will, from this day forward, release anything that has been keeping you from pursuing your dream. My wakeup call was when I realized that God was doing a new thing in my life, and I was afraid to not move with the Spirit. I felt that the timing for completing this project was right, and knew that if I did not accept my calling on this project, He would use someone else.

Sometimes we can wait too long and miss out on our blessings. If you feel that you have angered God by moving too slowly or not moving at all when you were called to do something, it's still not too late. Go to Him and ask for forgiveness; He's waiting on you. He wants to bless your life tremendously. Timing is everything, so don't tarry.

Finally, I pray that you accept the offer of God's Salvation which is the greatest gift of all and which will give you the *GREATEST VICTORY!* Remember, *Life Is Always in Progress... So Take the Brakes Off!*

"I have fought the good fight, I have finished the race,
I have kept the faith."
~~2 Timothy 4:7

Life is always in progress...so take the breaks off

Acknowledgements

First and foremost, I would like to thank my lovely mother, Ruby Lee Hunter. Everything that I am, I owe to this wonderful woman. Her strength, hard work, wisdom and encouragement made me what I am today.

I would also like to give thanks to my family and friends for supporting me in this project.

I hesitate to name other's that were very instrumental in making this project a success for concern of leaving someone out. If so, please believe that this was not done intentionally.

Special thanks to: Publisher, Ronnie Wells; Self-Publishing Assistant, Conchata Wells; Editors, Racquel Mitchell and Connie Sandidge; Proofreaders, Nekeisha Hardy, Michelle Miller, Una Richards, Deborah Abernathy and Shirley Spearman; Inspiration and Encouragement, Aunt Lillie Thomas, Eunice Arnold, Quincy Fulton and Tanji; Public Relations, Cameca Fenderson; Technology, Gregory Cole and Terra Smiley; Program Décor, Delores Arline and Deidre Stokes; Community Support, Donna Dees, James Collins. Special Acknowledgment to my leadership team at Bethune Middle School, Roslyn Mafico, Michael Williamson, Linda Johnson, James McNealey, Anthony Davis, Officer Gilley, Larry Williams, Debra Abernathy, Alain Davis, D'Adrieen Thompson, Vanette Jordan, Anthony Rutledge. Last but not least, Michelle and James Miller.

About the Author

Loretta H. Browning was born and raised in Atlanta, Georgia. She has two daughters and five grandchildren. She retired from DeKalb County School System in 2004.

Loretta is a successful business owner and devout community organizer. She started her gift basket company, "Simply Blessed Gift Creations," in 1997 and started a community organization, "Grassroots Neighborhood Connect" which has a mission of creating a stronger bond between neighbors, local business owners, schools and churches, in 2008.

Loretta resides in Lithonia, GA, and is a member of New Life Baptist Church.

For speaking engagements or book signings go to www.simplyblessed.net.